WRITTEN BY:

JAMIE MUNRO

WEBSITE:

HTTP://WWW.ENDYOURIF.COM

To my wife who supported me and our children during the many hours
of work required to put this book together!

CONTENTS

PREFACE

WHO IS THIS BOOK FOR?

This book was written by a web developer for web developers. It is written in a fashion where it will be useful for beginning web developers and also help advanced web developers learn more.

To ensure you are not completely lost, knowledge of PHP, Javascript, HTML, and CSS are required. A basic understanding of Object Oriented Programming (OOP) is useful, but not 100 percent required.

Whether you are an advanced web developer or a beginner looking to learn CakePHP, this book promises to help you build simple and complex web sites, quickly and easily.

The goal of this book is to provide a wide variety of useful functionality that is required by most websites today. In the final chapter, we will take all that we've learned and create one final large project.

During this process, I will instill my knowledge in taking a project from start to finish including creating a scope of work to ensure we have accomplished our target goals.

By the end of this book, you should be able to build fully functional websites using CakePHP. Hopefully, you should also be able to cut your development time at least in half, if not more!

ABOUT THE AUTHOR

I have been developing websites both personally and professionally for the past 15 years. During this time I've helped engineer dozens of small and large projects using CakePHP as the framework.

The ideas and methodologies behind this book all stem from my experience with providing quality web applications to my clients.

I am well versed in many web technologies as well as several software development languages. My brain is constantly working as I'm always looking to better myself as I strive to continue my role as lead developer.

For more information, visit my blog at http://www.endyourif.com

SPECIAL NOTE ABOUT VERSION

I feel it is important to share this special note about the version of CakePHP used for this book. Originally this book was written during version 1.2. However, it has taken some time to complete and format this book for print. During this time, CakePHP has released version 1.3 and even 2.0 in development mode.

All of the code samples were originally done for version 1.2, so if you are using version 1.3 you may notice some subtle differences. Fear not, all of the code should function without issue in version 1.3.

You will notice that there is a special last chapter that has been added discussing the upgrade process from version 1.2 to 1.3 and how extremely pain*less* it was!

CHAPTER 1

WHAT IS CAKEPHP

CakePHP was created in 2005 and has evolved quite a bit over the past six years. The founder of CakePHP is Larry E. Masters. It is thanks to this man and his team of developers that CakePHP has such a great framework. In this chapter, we will discuss the technology and architecture behind CakePHP to help provide us an understanding of what CakePHP offers us as developers.

OBJECTIVES

- Understand the technology behind CakePHP

- Learn about the Model-View-Controller architecture

- Learn about the Object-Relational Mapping

- Learn how CakePHP helps us develop faster through Rapid Application Development

CakePHP is a framework built with and for PHP. CakePHP allows web developers the use of MVC (Model-View-Controller) and ORM (Object-Relational Mapping) to rapidly build web applications.

MODEL-VIEW-CONTROLLER

To begin understanding how to build CakePHP websites, it is important to understand what the framework is based on. Like most frameworks, CakePHP is based on the architecture called Model-View-Controller, or its better known acronym MVC.

TIP: Did you know that MVC was originally called "THING-MODEL-VIEWEDITOR"?

MVC makes it easy to distinguish between business logic and the visual appearance of our websites without one affecting the other.

The Model of the MVC represents the data layer of our application. The data can vary in many ways. It can be an XML file or a CSV file, but more often than not, a model relates to a table in a database.

The model allows us to interact with the data, but not directly. The framework acts on our behalf and returns the data that we need.

The View of the MVC represents the visual or "view" layer of our application. Like the model layer, the view can vary as well. It can output XML, PDF documents, or any other visual data; most use it to output HTML (Hyper Text Markup Language). Views are often referred to as templates.

Views can be a one-to-one relationship with a webpage you are viewing or it can be made up of several different views. If the elements being displayed are used in several places, one view would be created and called from the other places wishing to display it. This is a form of object oriented programming (OOP).

The Controller of the MVC represents the business logic. Controllers are also used to interact with both the Model and the View. The two should never interact directly and a controller should always mediate the interaction.

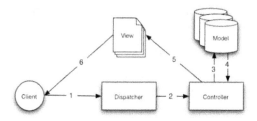

Figure 1: CakePHP's MVC Pattern

For example, if we have a view that displays information about a user, our controller would request the data from the user model. The model would fetch and return the information to the controller. The controller would then, if needed, process the data and continue by passing it to use in our view. Our view would then present the information in a useable format to the web browser.

Controllers are often referred to as the "brains" of the operation. While this is very true, I am a strong believer in segregating my code into small functions. This ensures that our controllers are neat and tidy.

As a newbie to CakePHP or MVC in general, it's quite easy to place *everything* in our controller. However, after time you will come to learn, and appreciate, that the cleaner we keep our controllers, the easier it will be to maintain and re-use code.

This will be explained in more detail when we discuss components in chapter 6.

OBJECT-RELATIONAL MAPPING

ORM is a technique that creates a "virtual object database". CakePHP uses ORM to convert our database tables into objects that we can manipulate through code without having to interact directly with our database.

It also makes it easier to tie our related tables together and be able to manipulate those in an easy fashion.

For example, let's pretend we have a table of companies. A company can have 0 or more employees. In our employees table, we would create a foreign key to our company. When we create our models in CakePHP, we tell it which tables are related to each other and how.

CakePHP uses this relationship not only to correctly retrieve the data from our database, but also to build our objects of requested data.

With the example above, if we were to use CakePHP to retrieve all companies and employees for each company, CakePHP would perform our query and process the results. Thus creating an array of data organized first by company and then by the company's associated employees as a sub array.

This is an extremely useful tool that saves us hours of time having to organize and output our data ourselves.

An example array from CakePHP is displayed below.

```
1.    Array (

2.        [0] => Array (

3.            'Company' => Array (

4.                'name' => 'XYZ Holding',
```

```
5.            'address' => '123 Holding Street',

6.            'city' => 'Ottawa',

7.            'state' => 'ON',

8.            'country' => 'Canada'

9.        )

10.       'Employee' => Array (

11.           [0] => Array(

12.               'name' => 'John Doe'

13.           )

14.       )

15.   )

16. )
```

As you can see in the example above, CakePHP uses ORM to manipulate our data into organized arrays that allow us to access and manipulate it as we need. Understanding this now is extremely important to understand how we will create our simple and complex websites later.

If the above array was stored in a variable called $companies, we could use the following code to output a list of companies and their employees:

```
1.   <?php foreach ($companies as $company):?>

2.   <h1><?php echo $company['Company']['name'];?></h1>
```

```
3.    <ul>

4.        <?php foreach ($company['Employee'] as
           $employee):?><li><?php echo $employee['name']</li>

5.        <?php endforeach;?>

6.    </ul>

7.    <?php endforeach;?>
```

The above code would be placed in a view. As you may notice, we are always using PHP's long format of, e.g. <?php echo 'test';?> instead of <?='test';?>. This is not a mandatory requirement; however, most PHP frameworks encourage this practice to improve readability in our templates.

WHAT ELSE CAN CAKEPHP DO

Along with its MVC framework and ORM capabilities, CakePHP offers us a lot of great and useful functionality to help simplify many aspects of website development.

As you will see in all future chapters, CakePHP has created many useful "helper" classes, as well as "component" classes that make all of the tedious web development tasks easy and virtually bug free. For example, CakePHP provides an excellent helper to create pagination in any view. This saves us hours of time performing the math to determine the number of pages and most importantly, testing if it is done correctly. Prior to each release of CakePHP, the helpers and components are put through rigorous testing.

Because CakePHP is built with OOP in mind, it provides us the ability to easily create and use our own helpers and components as well. This makes our life extremely easy; it also makes code that much easier to re-use.

Later on in the book, we will go into further detail about helpers and components. For now it is just important to know that CakePHP offers many of them and take advantage of all the tools provided to us.

> **TIP:** My first CakePHP project was a combination website and Facebook application. CakePHP was an excellent candidate to create one set of code with conditional processing for the Facebook application.

SUMMARY

As a beginner to CakePHP, take the time to learn the various built-in helpers before you resort to writing custom code. I've seen a lot of time wasted by someone creating a wheel that already existed, worst of all, it wasn't even round! This may seem time consuming while you are learning, but stick with it during this phase and the benefits will pay off tenfold later.

When I first started developing, I was too stubborn to learn the syntax of using the built-in HTML helper to create a link. Rather than spending the extra 2-3 minutes early on to review the syntax, I reverted to writing the HTML myself.

Over a year later, we need to update *every* link and append an attribute to it for the Facebook application. If all of our links were done using the HTML helper, we would have been done in about 5 minutes. Because we didn't, we spent one week, yes over 40 hours of time, converting all HTML links to use the HTML helper.

Learn from my mistake and trust me on this one, it was not a fun week!

CHAPTER 2

HOW TO SETUP CAKEPHP

Thus far we have been learning what's behind CakePHP. It's now time to get our hands dirty and install CakePHP for the first time. Throughout the remainder of the book we will build off of this base project.

OBJECTIVES

- Learn about CakePHP requirements

- Download and setup CakePHP

- Configuring CakePHP for the first time

- Creating a database connection

- Overview of CakePHP's folder structure

The developers of CakePHP have done a great job at making it extremely easy to setup CakePHP and begin developing; I guess that is why they call it Rapid Application Development.

The first step when setting up a CakePHP project is to download it. Visit http://www.cakephp.org. At the time of writing this book, there is a download button displayed prominently on the homepage. Click the button and select what type of file you would like to download, e.g. ZIP, DMG, etc...

If you will be installing CakePHP on a Mac, select the "dmg" file. Windows users should select the "zip" file. The 'Nix users should select the "gz" or "bz2" based on their preference.

SETUP AND CONFIGURATION

To continue with the next steps, you must have a web server configured and running with an available database server. In my case, because I am running Windows, I am using XAMPP. It's a great, simple, and an easy setup. It provides me with a fully functional Apache, PHP, and Mysql setup. Visit http://sourceforge.net/projects/xampp/ to download and install a copy today.

The next step is somewhat dependant on your setup. If you are running a web server locally, extract the files from your download into a new sub folder under your web root directory. Or, if you require a virtual host, set it up and extract the files into the directory for your new virtual host.

> **TIP:** CakePHP uses Apache's rewrite module. If you are hosting the application on a virtual host, you may need to alter the .htaccess files shipped with CakePHP. The solution that I have successfully used in the past is to add the following "RewriteBase /" to the .htaccess file in the root of the site, as well as the app folder, and finally in the webroot folder under the app folder.

Once you have extracted the files, open up a web browser and navigate to the URL where you extracted the files. For example, if you created a new folder on your local web server called "HelloWorld", you would navigate to http://localhost/HelloWorld. Assuming everything went well, you should see a page similar to Figure 2 below.

Figure 2: A Basic CakePHP Installation

As you can see by our screenshot, we have a couple of problems to correct. Items in yellow are just warnings, but a good idea to resolve. If you see items in red, that means there was an error.

> **TIP:** You may see a red message indicating your "tmp" directory is not writable. To fix this issue, allow the web server to have write permission to the following folder and its sub folders: <htdocs>/HelloWorld/app/tmp

The first warning we have above is telling us that our Security.salt value is still the default value. To resolve this issue, open the file: <htdocs>/HelloWorld/app/config/core.php in your favorite PHP editor. Search for the words "Security.salt". The next step we can accomplish a couple of different ways. The first way is to simply randomly change the string ourselves. Or, the more secure way is generate your own key using some PHP code and the MD5 function. For the purpose of this book, solution one will work.

After you have updated the string, save the file and reload the web page in your browser, the yellow message will disappear. At this point, we still have one more warning informing us that we do not have a database configuration file created.

DATABASE CONFIGURATION

Since 95% of web sites use a database of some sort, let's create one for our HelloWorld application. We won't do anything with it, but we should set it up now for future chapters.

Using your favorite database configuration tool, create a new database on your server called "HelloWord". If you've installed XAMPP, PHPMyAdmin it is most likely automatically installed for you and can be accessed by: http://localhost/phpmyadmin/

Now that we've created our database, let's create our database configuration file. In the folder: <htdocs>/HelloWorld/app/config there should be a file called "database.php.default". Rename the file to "database.php" and open the file in your editor.

```
1.   class DATABASE_CONFIG {

2.       var $default = array(

3.           'driver' => 'mysql',

4.           'persistent' => false,

5.           'host' => 'localhost',

6.           'login' => 'root',

7.           'password' => '',
```

```
8.          'database' => 'HelloWorld',

9.          'prefix' => '',

10.    );

11.

12.    var $test = array(

13.         'driver' => 'mysql',

14.         'persistent' => false,

15.         'host' => 'localhost',

16.         'login' => 'user',

17.         'password' => 'password',

18.         'database' => 'test_database_name',

19.         'prefix' => '',

20.    );

21.  }
```

At this stage, we can ignore the $test array and just update the $default array. Save your database.php file and reload your web page. We should no longer see any yellow messages and just two green messages.

> **TIP:** If you see a red error message for your database configuration, double check your host, login, password, and database name above. Also, if you are not using Mysql, ensure you update your driver from "mysql" to your driver type.

CAKEPHP'S FOLDER STRUCTURE

Before we begin writing any code, it's important to understand CakePHP's folder structure. It might seem a little confusing at first, but don't worry, you will be an expert in no time!

Let's start at the top-most level. In this level we have three folders: app, cake, and vendors. The app folder is where we will place all of our code. The cake folder contains all of the code to run the framework. Ideally, we should never need to modify this code. If you do need to, it's best to "override" the file in the app folder. I'll go into more detail about this shortly. To be honest, I do not know why there is a vendors folder at the top level. I've only used the one inside of the app folder.

At first glance, the app folder is quite daunting. It contains 10 folders: config, controllers, locale, models, plugins, tests, tmp, vendors, views, and webroot. During the initial setup, or module additions, we will need a wider variety of the folders. However, for the most part, we use just the controllers, models, and views folders.

The config folder, as the name implies, contains the various configuration files that CakePHP provides us to setup and run our CakePHP application.

The controllers folder is where we house our code to control the interaction between our database and our visual display. Inside the controllers folder is another folder called "components". Components are object classes. CakePHP comes with several prebuilt components such as, email, session, etc... Components allow us to remove some logic that might exist in our controllers so we may keep them neat and tidy or simply because we want to re-use this code elsewhere in our project.

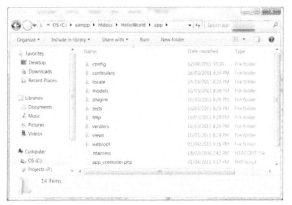

Figure 3: Typical "app" folder structure

The locale folder is where we store our language definition files. By default an eng folder resides inside of it. If we were to create a "fre" folder for French (or another language preference), it would allow us to place a language file inside that would contain all of our French translations. CakePHP has done an excellent job making our life easy if we wanted to make a multi-lingual site.

The models folder is where we place our code to control the interaction to our database. We create one file per database table. The standard rule of thumb is to create our tables plural and then our model is the singular of the name. For example, if we have a table called users, we would create a user.php file that would contain our User class to interact with that particular table.

The plugins folder is a neat feature about CakePHP that allows developers to package models, controllers, and views as a plugin that snaps in to other CakePHP projects.

TIP: Many excellent user created plugins are available from CakePHP's bakery: http://bakery.cakephp.org/articles/category/plugins

The tests folder is where we put our test cases. CakePHP has created the ability to easily create unit and web testing. To accomplish this, you would need to download SimpleTest and install it, and then begin writing your own test cases or using CakePHP's built-in test case scenarios. Unfortunately we don't have enough time in this book to cover test cases. If you are serious about testing, I would purchase a book solely focused on the topic for best results.

> **TIP:** Download SimpleTest from: http://simpletest.sourceforge.net/ and install it in your vendors folder.

The tmp directory is as it states, it contains all of our temporary files. This directory has several sub directories to divide the various temporary files that are stored. This includes, but is not limited to; log files, persistent model data, and cached data.

The vendors directory allows us to import 3rd party libraries and use them in our code. An example of a vendor would be the Facebook developers API. We could download the library and store it in a sub directory under vendors. In our project we would import the vendor and be able to begin using the library.

The views directory doesn't contain any files directly. Instead it contains many sub directories, one for each controller, plus several default directories. Inside the directories is where we store our view files that contain our HTML and other output sources.

Finally, the webroot directory contains several sub directories to help us keep our CSS, files, and Javascript files neatly organized. This directory also contains index.php which is the file that is loaded with each page request to instantiate CakePHP and its various features.

SUMMARY

I hope you now have a thorough understanding of CakePHP itself and its directory structure. In the next chapter we begin by creating our first functional CakePHP project.

CHAPTER 3

CREATING YOUR FIRST CAKEPHP WEBSITE

In the last chapter we performed a few minor changes to code; it's now time to begin creating something useful. Today's lesson will begin to demonstrate how rapidly we can develop in CakePHP.

OBJECTIVES

- Create a user registration form

- Learn about CakePHP's form validation

In this chapter, we will advance our HelloWorld application that we created in the previous chapter.

One of the most common website functionality in many of today's websites is user registration and that is exactly what we will be creating today. In future chapters, we will advance on the user registration and include user authentication.

DATABASE CREATION

To begin, let's create a standard users table. In your database editor, create a new table called users and add several fields. Ensure you add a field for email address and password; we will be using these later for our authentication. Below is a sample CREATE TABLE statement that I have used:

```
1.   CREATE TABLE `users` (

2.      `id` int(10) unsigned NOT NULL auto_increment,
```

3.   `first_name` varchar(45) NOT NULL,

4.   `last_name` varchar(45) NOT NULL,

5.   `email` varchar(150) NOT NULL,

6.   `password` varchar(45) NOT NULL,

7.   `address` varchar(45) default NULL,

8.   `address2` varchar(45) default NULL,

9.   `city` varchar(45) default NULL,

10.   `state` varchar(45) default NULL,

11.   `zipcode` varchar(10) default NULL,

12.   `country` varchar(45) default NULL,

13.   `created` datetime default NULL,

14.   `modified` datetime default NULL,

15.   PRIMARY KEY (`id`)

16.   ) ENGINE=InnoDB DEFAULT CHARSET=latin1;

MODEL, CONTROLLER, AND VIEW

The next step is to create our model. In the app\models directory, create a new file called user.php. Below is an example of a basic user model:

1.   <?php

2.   class User extends AppModel {

```
3.      var $name = 'User';

4.   }

5.   ?>
```

Next up is our controller. In the app\controllers directory, create a new file called users_controller.php. Below is an example of a basic users controller:

```
1.   <?php

2.   class UsersController extends AppController {

3.      var $name = 'Users';

4.      var $helpers = array('Html', 'Form');

5.   }
```

The next thing we need to do is create a new folder to store our views for our users controller. In the app\views directory, create a new sub directory called users. Inside of that directory, create a blank file called add.ctp. This is where we will create our form for the registration.

Let's do that now, below is a very basic add.ctp file that contains one form input per field in the database:

```
1.   <?php echo $form->create('User');?>

2.   <?php

3.      echo $form->input('first_name');

4.      echo $form->input('last_name');
```

```
5.      echo $form->input('email');

6.      echo $form->input('password');

7.      echo $form->input('address');

8.      echo $form->input('address2');

9.      echo $form->input('city');

10.     echo $form->input('state');

11.     echo $form->input('zipcode');

12.     echo $form->input('country');

13. ?>

14. <?php echo $form->end('Submit');?>
```

In the above example, the first thing we do is create our new form. We accomplish this by using CakePHP's FormHelper class and the create function.

The next thing we do is use the input function, once per field. You may notice that we have not included the id, created, and modified fields. The id field is automatically incremented for us by the database server and CakePHP will automatically set the created and modified date for us each time we save data, if the fields exist.

In your browser, you should now be able to navigate to http://localhost/HelloWorld/users/add and you should see our basic form. It won't save yet, but don't worry, we are getting to that.

To allow us to save data, we need to create a new function in our users_controller.php file called "add". Let's do that now:

```
1.   function add() {

2.      if (!empty($this->data)) {

3.         $this->User->create();

4.         if ($this->User->save($this->data)) {

5.            $this->Session->setFlash('User successfully created');

6.            $this->redirect('/');

7.         } else {

8.            $this->Session->setFlash('There was an error saving the
       user');

9.         }

10.     }

11.  }
```

The first thing this function does is check if there is content in our $this->data variable. When we use the FormHelper, CakePHP automatically populates this variable for us with data from the $_POST and $_GET variable.

If the variable has some data, e.g. the form was submitted, it calls the create function. This tells the model that our save will be creating a new record. We do this on the next line. We place the call to the save function in an if statement because if our validation (or any other error occurs during the save process) fails it will return false. If it returns false, we display an error message for the user. If it returns true, we display a success message to the user and redirect back to the homepage.

If you now go back to http://localhost/HelloWorld/users/add and submit the form, a new user will be created and saved in our database. If you didn't enter any data in you will notice that most of our fields are empty.

DATA VALIDATION

This is not something we want to allow. Let's change this by adding validation to our form. CakePHP makes it extremely simple for us. To do this, we need to modify our user model. Below is an example validation array:

```
1.   var $validate = array(

2.      'first_name' => array('notempty'),

3.      'last_name' => array('notempty'),

4.      'email' => array(

5.          'email' => array(

6.              'rule' => 'email',

7.              'required' => true,

8.              'message' => 'Please enter a valid email address'

9.          ),

10.         'unique' => array(

11.             'rule' => 'isUnique',

12.             'message' => 'The email address already exists in our system'

13.         )
```

```
14.    ),

15.    'password' => array('notempty'),

16.  );
```

This example contains a fair number of rules. We start by indicating that the first and last name fields cannot be empty. We then proceed to ensure that our email address field is a valid email. CakePHP contains several regular expressions that are used quite frequently. We also tell CakePHP to ensure that our email address is unique in our database. This is a bit of forward planning for our authentication system. Finally, we ensure our password is not empty.

If you visit http://localhost/HelloWorld/users/add again and click the form without inputting any information, you should see several error messages.

Figure 4: Example error messages

Challenge: To help you learn more about validation, update our validation array to ensure that Address, City, State, Zip Code, and Country are mandatory as well. Hint: for the zip code, we also want to ensure it is a valid zip code. CakePHP offers a built-in regular expression. Search it out at http://book.cakephp.org.

SUMMARY

Was that easy enough for you? I know at first it might seem a bit complicated with the various files that you need to work with. But, trust me, once you begin to gain a better understanding, you will find that these simple tasks become easier and easier and take you less and less time.

CHAPTER 4

HOW TO USE THE BAKERY

Once you've created a few models, views, and controllers, you will begin to find these tasks very repetitive and extremely mundane. In this chapter, we'll learn how we can turn 5 to 10 keystrokes into a complete website application.

OBJECTIVES

- Understand CakePHP's bakery

The bakery, this might be CakePHP's best feature. I know it's difficult to pick just one, but the bakery can save you many hours of time. The bakery allows us to run through a simple process, press a few keys, and create all of our code for us!

DATABASE CONFIGURATION

To show you the true nature and beauty of the bakery, let's create two new tables. The tables will be called albums and photos. Below are two example CREATE TABLE statements, one for each table:

1. CREATE TABLE `albums` (

2.   `id` int(10) unsigned NOT NULL auto_increment,

3.   `user_id` int(10) unsigned NOT NULL,

4.   `name` varchar(45) NOT NULL,

5.   `photo_count` int(10) unsigned NOT NULL,

6.   `created` datetime default NULL,

7.   `modified` datetime default NULL,

8.   PRIMARY KEY (`id`)

9.   ) ENGINE=InnoDB DEFAULT CHARSET=latin1;

10.

11.   CREATE TABLE `photos` (

12.   `id` int(10) unsigned NOT NULL auto_increment,

13.   `album_id` int(10) unsigned NOT NULL,

14.   `caption` varchar(45) NOT NULL,

15.   `image` varchar(150) NOT NULL,

16.   `created` datetime default NULL,

17.   `modified` datetime default NULL,

18.   PRIMARY KEY (`id`)

19.   ) ENGINE=InnoDB DEFAULT CHARSET=latin1;

Now that we have our tables, we can begin baking our files. We will need command line access to complete the next part.

TIP: Windows users click the Start Menu and select Run. In the Run dialog, enter "cmd" without the quotes, and press enter.

With the command prompt (or terminal window) open, navigate to your HelloWorld project. In my case it would be: cd \xampplite\htdocs\HelloWorld <enter>

RUNNING THE BAKERY

To run the bakery you perform the following command: cake\console\cake bake

> **TIP:** If you receive an error regarding cannot find PHP, this means that your executable path does not contain the PHP.exe in it. To solve this you will need to either add the directory where the PHP binary is installed or edit the batch file "cake\console\cake.bat" to include the full path to the PHP.exe.

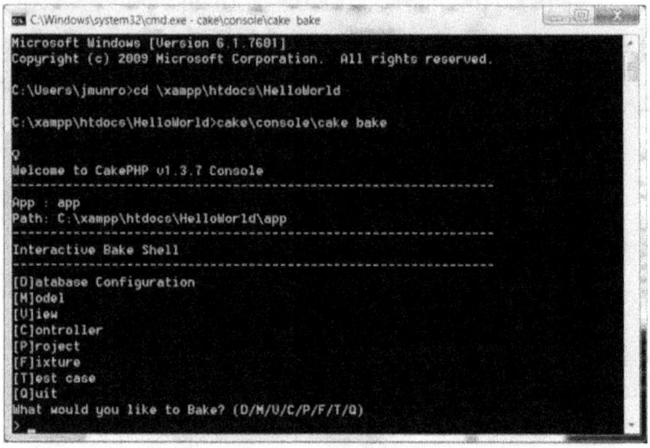

Figure 5: Welcome screen to the Cake Bakery

As you can see by the options, the bakery allows us to configure our database connection, create models, create views, create controllers, and create projects. For the purpose of this chapter, we will only be creating models, views, and controllers.

MODEL CREATION

Let's start by baking our models. In the command prompt, type **M** and press enter. The bakery now asks us which database configuration it should use. The default database configuration is selected automatically, so we can simply push enter to continue.

The bakery makes the connection to our database and lists the three tables that we have created in our HelloWorld database: Album, Photo, and User. Let's start by baking our Album model. Input **1** and press enter. Cake now asks us if we would like to supply validation and the default answer is yes. Since we do, simply press enter to continue. For each field we have 29 different validation options to choose from. We will be offered these same 29 options for each field in our table. CakePHP always attempts to pick the best one based on the column name and type.

We do not need validation in the id field. The default value is 29 (do not validate), so we can just press enter. Next up is our user_id field; the default is 21, numeric. Again, this correct, so we can press enter to move on. The default for name is 20, not empty, press enter to accept this. photo_count is set to 21 as well, press enter to continue. The last two fields: created and modified are defaulted to no validation, so press enter twice to accept these two defaults.

We have now completed capturing our validation rules. CakePHP now asks us if we would like to create associations (hasMany, hasOne, belongsTo, etc...). The default answer is yes, so press enter to continue.

> **TIP:** As of version 1.3, CakePHP now includes adding multiple validation rules to one field.

The bakery now reads the fields and the other table names and attempts to find our relationships for us. Because we've named our fields correctly, it asks us if we want Album to belong to User. To ensure proper associations when we want tables to be related, we need to create a foreign key with the <model name>_id, e.g. user_id. The default answer is yes; press enter to accept this relationship.

The bakery has also found our reverse relationship and that Album has many photos. Press enter to confirm this relationship. The bakery also asks us if an Album only has one Photo. Since we've already specified that albums can have many photos; type **n** and press enter.

CakePHP can no longer find any other associations so it will ask if we would like to manually specify anymore. The default answer is no. Press enter to continue.

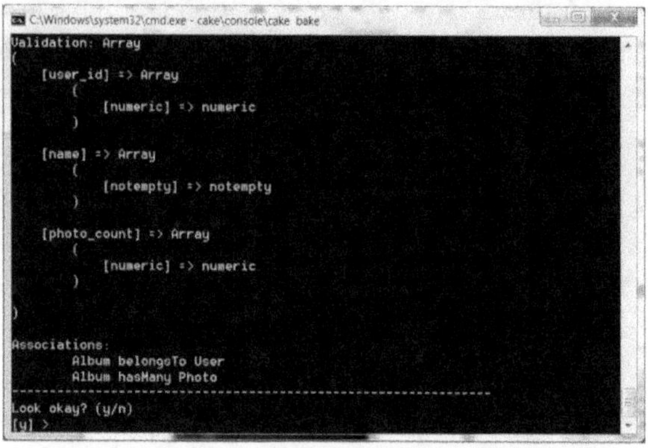

Figure 6: Summary of the Album model

Prior to saving the file, the bakery displays a summary and asks us if it looks correct. The default answer is yes, so press enter to complete the process and create the Album model.

After finishing the model, CakePHP also has the ability to create several test cases for your model. By default SimpleTest is not installed. It will ask if you wish to create the test cases. Because the default answer is yes, I normally press enter because you never truly know if you will install SimpleTest and use those test scenarios later.

Our model is now completed. If you browse to app\models, you should see a new file called album.php. Open it up and see what CakePHP creates automatically for you with a few simple questions!

```php
1.  <?php

2.  class Album extends AppModel {

3.      var $name = 'Album';

4.      var $validate = array(

5.          'user_id' => array('numeric'),

6.          'name' => array('notempty'),

7.          'photo_count' => array('numeric')

8.      );

9.

10. //The Associations below have been created with all possible keys,
    those that are not needed can be removed

11. var $belongsTo = array(

12.     'User' => array(

13.         'className' => 'User',

14.         'foreignKey' => 'user_id',

15.         'conditions' => '',

16.         'fields' => '',

17.         'order' => ''
```

```
18.    )

19.  );

20.

21.  var $hasMany = array(

22.     'Photo' => array(

23.          'className' => 'Photo',

24.          'foreignKey' => 'album_id',

25.          'dependent' => false,

26.          'conditions' => '',

27.          'fields' => '',

28.          'order' => '',

29.          'limit' => '',

30.          'offset' => '',

31.          'exclusive' => '',

32.          'finderQuery' => '',

33.          'counterQuery' => ''

34.     )

35.  );

36.  }

37.  ?>
```

CONTROLLER CREATION

Let's continue by creating the controller for the albums table. Type **C** and press enter. CakePHP uses our current database connection and retrieves three tables as the possible controllers we are able to create: Albums, Photos, and Users.

Type **1** and press enter so we can bake our albums controllers. The next step is a personal preference. The bakery asks us if we wish to bake our controller interactively. I normally select no because during this stage I don't know the various things that I will require and just want the basics created. Type **n** and press enter to skip the interactive mode.

The bakery now wants to know if we wish to include basic functions for: index(), add(), edit(), view(), and delete(). The default answer is yes, so press enter.

We are now asked if we wish to create admin routing. Admin routing is great if you wish to create a separate admin area, for example to manage users. For the purpose of this example, we will type **n** and press enter.

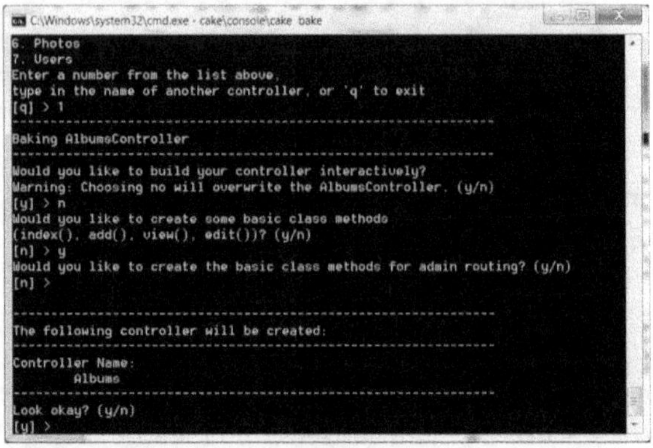

Figure 7: Summary of our albums controller

Just like when creating our model, before finishing and creating the file, CakePHP asks us to confirm the controller. The default answer is yes, so press enter to finish creating your controller.

The same question is asked again when we are finished with our model about creating test cases. Let's press enter in case we wish to create more test cases later.

Let's take a peek at the work the bakery has completed for us again. Browse to app\controllers.   You should see a new file called albums_controller.php. Open it up to see the fantastic work CakePHP has done for us.

```
1.   <?php

2.   class AlbumsController extends AppController {

3.       var $name = 'Albums';

4.       var $helpers = array('Html', 'Form');

5.       function beforeFilter() {
```

```
6.        parent::beforeFilter();

7.        if (!$this->Auth->user()) {

8.            $this->Auth->deny('add', 'edit', 'delete');

9.        }

10.  }

11.  function index() {

12.      $this->Album->recursive = 0;

13.      $this->set('albums', $this->paginate());

14.  }

15.  function view($id = null) {

16.      if (!$id) {

17.          $this->Session->setFlash(__('Invalid Album.', true));

18.          $this->redirect(array('action'=>'index'));

19.      }

20.      $this->set('album', $this->Album->read(null, $id));

21.  }

22.  function add() {

23.      if (!empty($this->data)) {

24.          $this->Album->create();

25.          if ($this->Album->save($this->data)) {

26.              $this->Session->setFlash(__('The Album has been saved',
         true));
```

```
27.             $this->redirect(array('action'=>'index'));

28.          } else {

29.             $this->Session->setFlash(__('The Album could not be
          saved. Please, try again.', true));

30.          }

31.       }

32.       $users = $this->Album->User->find('list');

33.       $this->set(compact('users'));

34.    }

35.    function edit($id = null) {

36.       if (!$id && empty($this->data)) {

37.          $this->Session->setFlash(__('Invalid Album', true));

38.          $this->redirect(array('action'=>'index'));

39.       }

40.       if (!empty($this->data)) {

41.          if ($this->Album->save($this->data)) {

42.             $this->Session->setFlash(__('The Album has been saved',
          true));

43.             $this->redirect(array('action'=>'index'));

44.          } else {

45.             $this->Session->setFlash(__('The Album could not be
          saved. Please, try again.', true));

46.          }
```

```
47.        }
48.        if (empty($this->data)) {
49.            $this->data = $this->Album->read(null, $id);
50.        }
51.        $users = $this->Album->User->find('list');
52.        $this->set(compact('users'));
53.    }
54.    function delete($id = null) {
55.        if (!$id) {
56.            $this->Session->setFlash(__('Invalid id for Album', true));
57.            $this->redirect(array('action'=>'index'));
58.        }
59.        if ($this->Album->del($id)) {
60.            $this->Session->setFlash(__('Album deleted', true));
61.            $this->redirect(array('action'=>'index'));
62.        }
63.    }
64. }
65. ?>
```

VIEW CREATION

Finally, let's create our views to accompany our index(), view(), add(), edit(), and delete() functions.

At the main bakery prompt, type **V** and press enter. The bakery provides us the same list of controllers previously found, type **1** and press enter to bake the views for the albums controller.

Before proceeding, CakePHP provides us a warning that we must create our model and controller before continuing. Since we've already done this, type **y** and press enter to confirm.

The bakery now asks us if we wish to create views for the admin routing. Since we did not create them with our controller, type **n** and press enter to skip.

That's it; the bakery has now created our four views for us. Browse to the app\views\albums folder and you will see the four new files: add.ctp, edit.ctp, index.ctp, and view.ctp.

SUMMARY

If anyone else is around, you may wish to covertly close your jaw from the amazement of the CakePHP bakery!

Prior to continuing to the next chapter, I would suggest baking the model, controller, and views for the photos table as well. After running through this process multiple times, you should be able to complete the three steps above in less than one minute. No joke!

CHAPTER 5

HOW TO SETUP AUTHENTICATION

Authentication is one of those things that have to be done in almost every interactive site we create. In today's chapter, we will explore how CakePHP provides an authentication component that we configure with a few parameters and how it completes the remaining process for us.

View the full source code online here: http://www.endyourif.com/login-system-with-cakephp-in-under-10-minutes/

OBJECTIVES

- Understand the authentication component

- Create and process login form

I enjoy developing with CakePHP for many different reasons. One of those reasons is the ease of setting up user authentication. This is an annoying task that you always have to do.

Like many things in CakePHP, they've done an excellent job making it easier. In this chapter, we will explore how easy it is to configure and setup.

LOGIN FORM

Let's begin by creating our login form. Create a new file called login.ctp inside of the app\views\users directory. Below is an example login form:

```
1.   <?php

2.      if ($session->check('Message.auth')) $session->flash('auth');

3.      echo $form->create('User', array('action' => 'login'));

4.      echo $form->input('email');

5.      echo $form->input('password');

6.      echo $form->end('Login');

7.   ?>
```

The next thing we need to do is create a couple of very basic functions inside of our users_controller.php. We need to create a blank login() function and a logout() function. The logout function clears our sessions and redirects us back to our logout page. A login() function is completely blank because CakePHP handles all of our validation for us.

```
1.   /**

2.   The AuthComponent provides the needed functionality

3.   for login, so you can leave this function blank.

4.   */

5.   function login() {}

6.

7.   function logout() {

8.      $this->redirect($this->Auth->logout());

9.   }
```

The next bit of code can be placed at the top of your users_controller.php if you plan to only require login when browsing the users controller. Because this is not normally the case, we are going to introduce a new file called the app_controller.php. Create a file called app_controller.php in the root of our app directory. You may have noticed that all of our controllers always extend the AppController. Because of this, we can place our code in the app controller and all other controllers will have the ability to invoke authentication.

AUTHENTICATION CONFIGURATION

Below is an example file with our authentication configured.

1. `<?php`

2. `class AppController extends Controller {`

3.

4. `var $components = array('Auth');`

5.

6. `function beforeFilter() {`

7. `$this->Auth->allow('*');`

8. `$this->Auth->userModel = 'User';`

9. `$this->Auth->fields = array('username' => 'email', 'password' => 'password');`

10. `$this->Auth->loginAction = array('admin' => false, 'controller' => 'users', 'action' => 'login');`

11. `$this->Auth->loginRedirect = array('controller' => 'users', 'action' => 'index');`

```
12.    }

13.

14.    function isAuthorized() {

15.        return true;

16.    }

17. }

18. ?>
```

Let's analyze each line of code in the beforeFilter function. The first line:

```
1.    $this->Auth->allow('*');
```

This is where we configure which actions to allow *without* requiring a user to be logged in.   An action is a public function inside of our controllers, e.g. the add() function we created in chapter 2. The * says to allow everything.   If you only wanted to allow index and add functionality, you would do the following:

```
1.    $this->Auth->allow('index', 'add');
```

The next line of code is:

```
1.    $this->Auth->userModel = 'User';
```

This line tells the authentication component to use the User model to check if it is a valid user. This is normally the default, but it can be changed to another table. For example, Admin, if you had a table called admins.

Next up is:

```
1.  $this->Auth->fields = array('username' => 'email', 'password' =>
    'password');
```

We are now configuring which fields in our users table to validate against. If you are using username and password, you can skip this line. Because we planned to use email, we need to specify that the email field is the username. It is important to note that if you are only changing one of the username or password fields you MUST pass both into the array.

Our next line is:

```
1.  $this->Auth->loginAction = array('admin' => false, 'controller' =>
    'users', 'action' => 'login');
```

This tells the authentication component to use the login function inside of the users controller. We also set admin to false. If we had admin routing set up and wanted to create a login for our administrators, we would then set this to true. This would allow our administrators to access the admin routing functions, e.g. admin_index().

Like the userModel field, the loginAction can be customized to use another controller and action.

The last line of code in the function is:

```
1.  $this->Auth->loginRedirect = array('controller' => 'users', 'action' =>
    'index');
```

This line tells the authentication component to redirect to the index function in the users controller. Like many of the other features, this can also be completely customized and redirect users to any controller and function we want.

Authentication is now successfully configured. We currently don't have too much control over which functions are protected and which are not. Let's explore adding this now.

PROTECTING OUR PAGES

Inside of our users controller, we don't have any functions that we need to protect. This means we can leave this one alone. The album and photo controllers that we created in the last chapter, however, contain several functions that we wish to ensure users are logged in for. Let's update these two controllers to prevent users from accessing the add, edit, and delete functions if they are not logged in.

Figure 8: Typical "not logged" in page

Open up both the album and photo controllers and place this function near the top.

```
1.   function beforeFilter() {

2.       parent::beforeFilter();

3.       if (!$this->Auth->user()) {

4.           $this->Auth->deny('add', 'edit', 'delete');

5.       }

6.   }
```

The first thing we do in this function is call our parent beforeFilter function. E.g. the one we previously created in the app_controller.php.

The next step is to deny the add, edit, and delete functions if there is no authenticated user.

SUMMARY

That's it; our authentication system is now setup. This can be easily moved from project-to-project very quickly each time allowing tried and true authentication on all of your projects.

CHAPTER 6

HOW TO CREATE AND USE COMPONENTS

Components offer us the ability to segregate some logic and data manipulation from our controllers. In today's chapter we will expand on our baked controllers from chapter 4. We will create a component that will upload an image and create a thumbnail of that image.

For another example of creating a component, visit: http://www.endyourif.com/stringextractcomponent-for-cakephp/

OBJECTIVES

- Further our knowledge of components

- Create our own component

- Upload a file and create a thumbnail version of an image

What is a component? A component is a PHP class. Component classes have the ability to extend other classes or they can be standalone classes.

UNDERSTANDING COMPONENTS

In the last chapter we actually used a component. To setup our login system, we used the authentication component. Let's begin by reviewing a portion of this component to gain a further understanding of them. To view the authentication component browse to: cake\libs\controller\components\auth.php. Below is an excerpt of the component (to save space, I've removed the detailed commenting from the code):

```php
1.   <?php

2.   class AuthComponent extends Object {

3.       var $_loggedIn = false;

4.       var $components = array('Session', 'RequestHandler');

5.       var $authenticate = null;

6.       var $authorize = false;

7.       var $ajaxLogin = null;

8.       var $userModel = 'User';

9.       var $userScope = array();

10.      var $fields = array('username' => 'username', 'password' =>
         'password');

11.      var $sessionKey = null;

12.      var $actionPath = null;

13.      var $loginAction = null;

14.      var $loginRedirect = null;

15.      var $logoutRedirect = null;

16.      var $object = null;

17.      var $loginError = null;

18.      var $authError = null;

19.      var $autoRedirect = true;

20.      var $allowedActions = array();

21.      var $actionMap = array(
```

```
22.      'index'                => 'read',

23.      'add'                  => 'create',

24.      'edit'                 => 'update',

25.      'view'                 => 'read',

26.      'remove'    => 'delete'

27.  );

28.  var $data = array();

29.  var $params = array();

30.  var $_methods = array();

31.  function initialize(&$controller) {

32.      $this->params = $controller->params;

33.      $crud = array('create', 'read', 'update', 'delete');

34.      $this->actionMap = array_merge($this->actionMap,
     array_combine($crud, $crud));

35.      $this->_methods = $controller->methods;

36.      $admin = Configure::read('Routing.admin');

37.      if (!empty($admin)) {

38.          $this->actionMap = array_merge($this->actionMap, array(

39.              $admin . '_index' => 'read',

40.              $admin . '_add'         => 'create',

41.              $admin . '_edit'  => 'update',

42.              $admin . '_view'  => 'read',
```

```
43.              $admin . '_remove'          => 'delete',

44.              $admin . '_create' => 'create',

45.              $admin . '_read'   => 'read',

46.              $admin . '_update'          => 'update',

47.              $admin . '_delete' => 'delete'

48.          ));

49.      }

50.      if (Configure::read() > 0) {

51.          App::import('Debugger');

52.          Debugger::checkSessionKey();

53.      }

54.  }

55.  ...

56. }

57. ?>
```

If you are familiar with PHP classes, this should look pretty familiar, if you are not, I'll give a brief overview.

The first thing that's done is create a class called AuthComponent and it extends Object. When we use our class we will need to instantiate it using the **new** keyword following by the class name:

```
1.    $this->Auth = new AuthComponent();
```

The next thing the script does is create several variables. If a variable begins with an underscore, it signifies that it is a protected variable. A protected variable should only be accessed by the class itself. What that means is that I should not attempt to access it like this:

1. $this->Auth->_privateVariable;

Normally when a class contains protected or private variables, the class will provide methods to both set and get the value of the variable.

After the component has created the various variables required, it creates functions. In the example above, a function with the name initialize has been created. We can access this function in our code by using the following command:

1. $this->Auth->initiliaze($this);

In the example above we pass **$this** to the function because it expects a controller, the example above assumes we are inside a controller using the auth component.

CREATING A COMPONENT

To further our learning, let's move on and create our very own component. You remember back in chapter 4 how we created the albums and photos controllers? Let's expand on the photos controller so we can actually upload files and save them to the hard drive. We will also get adventurous and create a thumbnail version of the image.

The first step is to create our component. Inside the app\controllers\components directory, create a new file called image_manipulation.php. Inside the file, we will define our class; create a couple of variables and the skeletons for our functions.

```php
1.   <?php

2.   class ImageManipulationComponent extends Object {

3.       var $_filepath;

4.       var $_filename;

5.

6.       function __construct() {

7.           // setup the location for us to save the files

8.           $this->_filepath = APP . 'webroot' . DS . 'files' . DS;

9.       }

10.

11.      function saveImage($fileinfo) {

12.

13.      }

14.

15.      function createThumbnail() {

16.

17.      }

18.  }
```

19. ?>

Ok, now we have our component created and two local variables. One will store the path for the files to be saved and the other will store the filename of the file that was uploaded.

IMPLEMENTING OUR COMPONENT

The next step is to update our app\views\photos\add.ctp to be able to upload files. We need to update the image field's input type to "file" and we need to change the encryption type on the form:

1.   <div class="photos form">

2.   <?php echo $form->create('Photo', array('enctype' => 'multipart/form-data'));?>

3.   <fieldset>

4.   <legend><?php __('Add Photo');?></legend>

5.   <?php

6.   echo $form->input('album_id');

7.   echo $form->input('caption');

8.   echo $form->input('image', array('type' => 'file'));

9.   ?>

10.   </fieldset>

11.   <?php echo $form->end('Submit');?>

12. </div>

```
13.  <div class="actions">

14.     <ul>

15.         <li><?php echo $html->link(__('List Photos', true),
        array('action'=>'index'));?></li>

16.     </ul>

17.  </div>
```

The highlighted code above shows the only two changes made from the original code created by the CakePHP bakery.

Figure 9: Add photo form

We now need to update our photos controller to invoke our component upon submission.   Open app\controllers\photos_controllers.php and make the following additions. At the top of the file import include our component:

```
1.    var $components = array('ImageManipulation');
```

Now we need to update our add function to call our component:

```
1.    function add() {

2.        if (!empty($this->data)) {

3.            // call our component

4.            $this->data['Photo']['image'] = $this->ImageManipulation-
              >saveImage($this->data['Photo']['image']);

5.

6.            $this->Photo->create();

7.            if ($this->Photo->save($this->data)) {

8.                $this->Session->setFlash(__('The Photo has been saved',
                  true));

9.                $this->redirect(array('action'=>'index'));

10.           } else {

11.               $this->Session->setFlash(__('The Photo could not be saved.
                  Please, try again.', true));

12.           }

13.       }

14.       $albums = $this->Photo->Album->find('list');
```

```
15.     $this->set(compact('albums'));

16.  }
```

In the function above, we call our saveImage function and pass in the file upload information. You will notice that the results of the function are stored in a variable; the reason for this is to ensure our filename is saved properly to the database.

FINISHING OUR COMPONENT

We are almost there, let's wrap this up by adding the necessary functionality to our component to save the file and resize it as a thumbnail. We will begin by updating our saveImage function first:

```
1.    function saveImage($fileinfo) {

2.        // store the name of the image to our local variable

3.        $this->_filename = $fileinfo['name'];

4.        // write the file to disk

5.        move_uploaded_file($fileinfo['tmp_name'], $this->_filepath . $this->_filename);

6.        // call our function to create our thumbnail

7.        $this->createThumbnail();

8.        // return back the filename to save it in the database

9.        return $this->_filename;

10.  }
```

This function is quite simple. We begin by saving the filename to our local variable. We then move the uploaded file from its temporary location to our permanent location. We then proceed to call our function to create our thumbnail (yet to be created). Finally, we return our filename to store in the database.

Let's now implement our function to create our thumbnail:

```
1.   function createThumbnail() {

2.      // get the extension of the file

3.      $ext = explode(".", $this->_filename);

4.      $ext = $ext[count($ext)-1];

5.

6.      // store our full filename

7.      $filename = $this->_filepath . $this->_filename;

8.      $t_filename = $this->_filepath . 'thumb_' . $this->_filename;

9.

10.     // set our max thumbnail width and height

11.     $xmax = 150;

12.     $ymax = 150;

13.

14.     if($ext == "jpg" || $ext == "jpeg")

15.        $im = imagecreatefromjpeg($filename);

16.     elseif($ext == "png")

17.        $im = imagecreatefrompng($filename);
```

```
18.     elseif($ext == "gif")

19.        $im = imagecreatefromgif($filename);

20.

21.     $x = imagesx($im);

22.     $y = imagesy($im);

23.

24.     // if our image is already smaller than our thumbnail, don't resize
        it, just save it

25.     if($x <= $xmax && $y <= $ymax) {

26.        copy($filename, $t_filename);

27.     } else {

28.        // if it is wider than tall, resize the height to make it
           proportional

29.        if($x >= $y) {

30.           $newx = $xmax;

31.           $newy = $newx * $y / $x;

32.        // otherwise resize the width to make it proportional

33.        } else {

34.           $newy = $ymax;

35.           $newx = $x / $y * $newy;

36.        }

37.

38.     $im2 = imagecreatetruecolor($newx, $newy);
```

```
39.    imagecopyresized($im2, $im, 0, 0, 0, 0, floor($newx),
       floor($newy), $x, $y);

40.

41.    // save the resized image

42.    if($ext == "jpg" || $ext == "jpeg")

43.        imagejpeg($im2, $t_filename);

44.    elseif($ext == "png")

45.        imagepng($im2, $t_filename);

46.    elseif($ext == "gif")

47.        imagegif($im2, $t_filename);

48.

49.    imagedestroy($im2);

50.    }

51.    imagedestroy($im);

52. }
```

The following function loads our saved image into an image resource. Based on the image type, we call the appropriate "imagecreatefrom" function. We then retrieve the width and height of the image. If the current image is smaller than our thumbnail, we copy the file instead of resizing it.

If the photo is larger, we calculate the new width and height and ensure it is proportional. To ensure it is proportional we determine if the image is landscape or portrait. Next, we copy the image resized to the new width and height.

Finally we save the file to the hard drive and clean up our image resources.

SUMMARY

My number one reason to create components is to ALWAYS keep my controllers as clean as possible. I've worked on many projects where all of the above code was inside the add() function of the photos controller. It makes it a real mess to work with. I prefer keeping my controllers as simple as possible and place my data manipulation or complex logic inside of components.

My rule of thumb is, if your function in your controller is more than 20 lines of code, you should probably create a component and move your logic in the component. It will make your code ten times more readable and potentially ten times easier to track down problems in your code or logic!

CHAPTER 7

HOW TO USE VENDORS

In the previous chapter we've allowed users to upload and save images. In today's lesson we will continue to advance our functionality and allow users to share an entire album of photos on their Facebook account. When we're done, we will have a one-click solution to share an entire album.

OBJECTIVES

- Import the Facebook API as a vendor

- Share our photos to an album on Facebook

Vendors are quite similar to components. However, vendors are normally 3rd party classes, libraries, or APIs. Using a vendor is quite simple; you must be getting tired of me saying how simple things are in CakePHP? To be frank, I never get tired of it; it's one of the many things that I love about it!

To demonstrate how to use vendors, we are going to continue advancing our album and photo management. How are we going to do that? We are going to incorporate the Facebook Developer API. If you are not familiar with Facebook applications, don't worry, they are not overly complicated.

ADDING A VENDOR

The first step is to sign up for the developer application on Facebook. Visit http://www.facebook.com/developers/ and follow the simple instructions to create a new application. Once you've created your application, download the PHP library. Extract the files to your app\vendors directory.

The purpose of our Facebook Application will be to allow users to share their albums on their Facebook account. To do this, let's update our app\views\albums\index.ctp and a new link to "Share on Facebook".

Figure 10: Albums listing page

Below is a small snippet of the updated index.ctp file. The new link has been highlighted:

1. `<td class="actions">`

2. `<?php echo $html->link(__('Share on Facebook', true), array('action'=>'share', $album['Album']['id'])); ?>`

3. `<?php echo $html->link(__('View', true), array('action'=>'view', $album['Album']['id'])); ?>`

4. `<?php echo $html->link(__('Edit', true), array('action'=>'edit', $album['Album']['id'])); ?>`

5. `<?php echo $html->link(__('Delete', true), array('action'=>'delete', $album['Album']['id']), null, sprintf(__('Are you sure you want to delete # %s?', true), $album['Album']['id'])); ?>`

6. `</td>`

USING A VENDOR

Alright, the easy part has been accomplished. The core of our work will go in a component; this component will interact with our vendor. Create a new file called facebook_api.php inside of your app\controllers\components directory.

1. `<?php`

2. `class FacebookApiComponent extends Object {`

3. `var $_instance;`

4. `var $_apikey;`

5. `var $_secretkey;`

6. `var $_userid;`

7. `var $_authToken;`

```
8.      var $_authTokenSecret;

9.      var $_albumid;

10.

11.     function __construct($apikey = null, $secretkey = null) {

12.        // include the vendor

13.        App::import('vendor', 'facebook-platform/php/facebook');

14.        $this->_apikey = $apikey;

15.        $this->_secretkey = $secretkey;

16.        // instantiate it

17.        $this->_instance = new Facebook($this->_apikey, $this->_secretkey);

18.        // get the logged in user

19.        $this->_userid = $this->_instance->require_login();

20.     }

21.

22.     function get_album_by_name($albumname) {

23.        // get all albums

24.        $albums = $this->_instance->api_client->photos_getAlbums($this->_userid, NULL);

25.        // loop through them all and check if it exists

26.        foreach ($albums as $album) {
```

```
27.          if ($album['name'] == $albumname)

28.              return $album['aid'];

29.      }

30.      return 0;

31.  }

32.

33.  function create_album($albumname) {

34.      $this->_albumid = $this->get_album_by_name($albumname);

35.      // if the album does not exist, create it

36.      if ($this->_albumid == 0) {

37.          // create album

38.          $results = $this->_instance->api_client-
             >photos_createAlbum($albumname, '', '', 'everyone', $this-
             >_userid);

39.          $this->_albumid = $results['aid'];

40.      }

41.  }

42.

43.  function upload_photo($filename) {

44.      // upload photo with album id

45.      $results = $this->_instance->api_client-
```

```
      >photos_upload($filename, $this->_albumid, '', $this->_userid);

46.    }

47.  }

48.  ?>
```

The following is our completed component. In our constructor we import our vendor and instantiate the Facebook vendor API. We call the vendors require_login() function. This ensures that our user is logged into Facebook. If the user is not logged in, Facebook will redirect them to their login page. Once they login, they will be redirected back to complete our process.

Next we have a function called get_album_by_name, this performs an API call with our vendor to retrieve the list of albums for that user. We loop through each one to see if our album already exists. If it does, we return the id for that album. If it doesn't we return 0.

Our next function is called create_album. This function calls our previous function to check if the album exists. If the album id is 0, we proceed to perform another API call to create a new album. The Facebook API returns us the new album id, which we store in our local variable.

The final function is called upload_photo. This function makes a final API call to upload our photo with the full path to our file.

See, I told you using vendors are quite simple. Let's finish off this process by making the necessary additions to our albums controller. Open app\controllers\albums_controller.php and add in our new function called share().

```
1.    function share($id) {

2.        if (!$id) {

3.            $this->Session->setFlash(__('Invalid id for Album', true));

4.            $this->redirect(array('action'=>'index'));

5.        }

6.

7.        // get the album and photo information

8.        $photos = $this->Album->find('all', array('conditions' =>
          array('Album.id' => $id)));

9.

10.       // load and instantiate our component

11.       App::import('Component', 'FacebookApi');

12.       $this->FacebookApi = new
          FacebookApiComponent('put_your_api_key_here',
          'put_your_secret_key_here');

13.

14.       // call our function to create the album if it does not exist

15.       $this->FacebookApi-
          >create_album($photos[0]['Album']['name']);

16.

17.       // loop through our files and upload the photo for each one

18.       foreach ($photos as $photo) {
```

```
19.        $this->FacebookApi->upload_photo(APP . 'webroot' . DS .
      'files' . DS . $photo['Photo']['image']);

20.    }

21. }
```

The first thing this function does is check to ensure we have a valid id. If we do not, we redirect back to the index page.

Next, we retrieve our album and photo information using the id passed to the function. We then import our component and instantiate the component with our API and Secret key. When we created our Facebook application, Facebook displays this information in the summary of the application. Copy and paste this data into our controller.

Once we've done that, we call our function to create our album. Once we've ensured our album exists, we loop through our photos and call the upload_photo function once per photo.

SUMMARY

Our CakePHP application is really starting to take shape. Let's recap what we've accomplished so far:

- Users can register for an account

- Adding, editing, and deleting albums and photos require users to login

- Photos get uploaded and a thumbnail is created

- Our albums can be shared on Facebook through the use of a vendor

CHAPTER 8

ACT LIKE A TREE

Previously making a category management system took a fair amount of time to build and test. It was always extremely tedious to ensure we built the hierarchy properly. CakePHP has eliminated this fear with a behavior that accomplishes the work for us.

In today's lesson we will use the Jquery Javascript library to implement an easy-to-use drag and drop process to manage an unlimited hierarchy of categories.

For the complete source code, visit: http://www.endyourif.com/drag-and-drop-category-management-with-cakephp/

OBJECTIVES

- Create a category management system

- Implement drag-and-drop

- Implement AJAX for a sleek management process

If you have explored the directory structure further, you may have noticed a sub folder called "behaviors" under the models directory. CakePHP has several built-in behaviors that are available to us: ACL, Containable, Translate, and Tree. Each behavior offers additional functionality to our models.

In this chapter, we will explore the tree behavior. The tree behavior offers us some great tools to manage data in a hierarchy format. We will use this feature to create an unlimited category/sub category tree.

DATABASE CONFIGURATION

Let's begin by creating our new table, categories:

```
1.   CREATE TABLE `categories` (

2.       `id` int(10) unsigned NOT NULL auto_increment,

3.       `name` varchar(255) NOT NULL,

4.       `parent_id` int(10) unsigned NOT NULL,

5.       `lft` int(10) unsigned NOT NULL,

6.       `rght` int(10) unsigned NOT NULL,

7.       PRIMARY KEY (`id`)

8.   ) ENGINE=InnoDB DEFAULT CHARSET=latin1;
```

The first three columns most likely look pretty familiar to you. The last two are most likely foreign. These columns store the left and right position of the category in the tree. Mysql has some built-in logic called MPTT. Mysql offers an excellent article about it here: http://dev.mysql.com/tech-resources/articles/hierarchical-data.html

It is not necessary to understand the underlying technology because CakePHP does all the work for us; we need to do very little.

After you've created your table, proceed to use the bakery to create your model, controller, and views for the categories table. If you require help with this, please refer back to "Chapter 4: How to use the bakery".

ADDING A BEHAVIOR

Everything baked? Perfect. The first thing we need to do is tell CakePHP that our category model will be using the tree behavior. Open app\models\category.php and add the following line beneath "var $name":

```
1.   var $actsAs = array('Tree');
```

Now, every time we call the save() and delete() functions on our category model, CakePHP will perform the additional work required to keep our tree hierarchy up-to-date.

The next thing we need to do is update our categories controller to perform a different type of find query. Open app\controllers\categories_controller.php and make the following changes to our index() function:

```
1.   function index() {

2.       $categories = $this->Category->find('threaded');

3.       $this->set(compact('categories'));

4.   }
```

The following code tells CakePHP to perform the work to create a linear array and indents each category level, e.g.

```
1.   Level 1a

    a.   Level 2a

    b.   Level 2b
```

2. Level 1b

    a.   Level 2c

        i.   Level 3a

This saves us a lot of time from having to perform the work ourselves to create our tree structure. Now we can simply output our categories using an unordered list. Let's do this now, open app\views\categories\index.ctp and update it to look as follows:

```
1.  <div class="categories index">

2.  <h2><?php __('Categories');?></h2>

3.  <ul>

4.     <?php foreach ($categories as $category): ?><li><?php echo $category['Category']['name'];?></li>

5.     <?php endforeach; ?>

6.  </ul>
```

With every save and delete statement, CakePHP ensures our tree is up-to-date. For example, if we insert a new record at the second level, it will automatically update the lft and rght values that define where the element exists in our tree.

FANCY CATEGORY MANAGEMENT

Let's take this one step further and make a really fancy AJAX'ed multi-level category management system.

To begin, we need to make a few small changes to our baked controller. Below is our altered code:

```php
1.   <?php

2.   class CategoriesController extends AppController {

3.       var $name = 'Categories';

4.       var $helpers = array('Html', 'Form', 'Javascript');

5.       var $components = array('RequestHandler');

6.

7.       function index() {

8.           // if it's ajax, set ajax layout

9.           if ($this->RequestHandler->isAjax())

10.              $this->layout = 'ajax';

11.          $categories = $this->Category->find('threaded');

12.          $this->set(compact('categories'));

13.      }

14.

15.      function add() {

16.          if (!empty($this->data)) {

17.              $this->Category->create();

18.              if ($this->Category->save($this->data)) {

19.                  $this->Session->setFlash(__('The Category has been saved', true));

20.                  //$this->redirect(array('action'=>'index'));
```

```
21.          } else {

22.              $this->Session->setFlash(__('The Category could not be
          saved. Please, try again.', true));

23.          }

24.      }

25.      $this->render(false);

26.  }

27.

28.  function edit($id = null) {

29.      if (!$id && empty($this->data)) {

30.          $this->Session->setFlash(__('Invalid Category', true));

31.          $this->redirect(array('action'=>'index'));

32.      }

33.      if (!empty($this->data)) {

34.          if ($this->Category->save($this->data)) {

35.              $this->Session->setFlash(__('The Category has been
          saved', true));

36.              //$this->redirect(array('action'=>'index'));

37.          } else {

38.              $this->Session->setFlash(__('The Category could not be
          saved. Please, try again.', true));

39.          }

40.      }
```

```
41.        if (empty($this->data)) {

42.            $this->data = $this->Category->read(null, $id);

43.        }

44.        $this->render(false);

45.    }

46.

47.    function delete($id = null) {

48.        if (!$id) {

49.            $this->Session->setFlash(__('Invalid id for Category', true));

50.            $this->redirect(array('action'=>'index'));

51.        }

52.        if ($this->Category->del($id)) {

53.            $this->Session->setFlash(__('Category deleted', true));

54.            $this->redirect(array('action'=>'index'));

55.        }

56.    }

57. }

58. ?>
```

The changes made are extremely minor. The first thing we do is update our index() function to check if the request is through AJAX. If it is, we tell our function to use the AJAX layout instead of the default layout. The reason for this is, when we need to reload our category list, we call the index() function through AJAX, but we don't want to re-display the entire layout, just the categories.

The two other changes exist in our add() and edit() functions. I've commented out the $this->redirect() lines. I've also added $this->render(false) because we don't actually want to load the add and edit view. This will be clear shortly.

DRAG AND DROP FUNCTIONALITY

That takes care of all of the controller changes. Let's focus on the views now. Below is our full copy of app\views\categories\index.ctp. It's quite extensive because it's loaded with Javascript. Normally, I would place this code in a separate Javascript file; however, for the purpose of this example it's in one large file for simplicities sake.

```php
1.   <?php

2.   $javascript->link(array('jquery', 'jquery-ui'), false);

3.   ?>

4.   <script>

5.   $(document).ready(function(){

6.       //set up the droppable list elements

7.       $("ul li").droppable({

8.           accept: ".ui-draggable",

9.           hoverClass: 'droppable-hover',

10.          greedy: true,

11.          tolerance: 'pointer',

12.          drop: function(ev, ui) {

13.              var dropEl = this;
```

```
14.             var dragEl = $(ui.draggable);

15.

16.             // get category id

17.             var parent_id = this.id.substring(9);

18.

19.             // get category name

20.             var category_name = $(dragEl.find("span").get(0)).html();

21.

22.             if (!isNaN(parent_id) && category_name.length > 0) {

23.                 var data;

24.                 var url = "categories/";

25.

26.                 // see if we are adding or editing

27.                 if (dragEl.attr("id").substring(0, 9) == "category_") {

28.                     // get the current id

29.                     var id = dragEl.attr("id").substring(9);

30.                     data = { 'data[Category][id]': id,
         'data[Category][name]': category_name,
         'data[Category][parent_id]': parent_id };

31.                     url += "edit";

32.                 } else {

33.                     data = { 'data[Category][name]': category_name,
         'data[Category][parent_id]': parent_id };
```

```
34.                 url += "add";

35.            }

36.

37.             // post to our page to save our category

38.             $.post(url, data, function() {

39.                 $.get("categories/index", function (data) {
        destroyDraggable(); $("#content").html(data); setupDraggable(); });

40.             });

41.        }

42.     }

43.  });

44.

45.  setupDraggable();

46. });

47.

48. function updateDragBox() {

49.   $($("#ui-
      draggable").find("span").get(0)).html($("#CategoryName").val());

50. }

51.

52. function setupDraggable() {

53.    $("#ui-draggable").draggable({

54.       containment: '#categories',
```

```
55.        stop: function(e,ui) {

56.            $(this).animate({ left: 0, top:0 }, 500);

57.            $(this).html('');

58.        }

59.    });

60.    $("#category_0").find("li").draggable({

61.        containment: '#categories',

62.    });

63. }

64.

65. function destroyDraggable() {

66.    $("#ui-draggable").draggable('destroy');

67.    $("#category_0").find("li").draggable('destroy');

68. }

69. </script>

70. <style>

71. #categories {

72.    padding: 1em 0.5em;

73.    width: 90%;

74. }

75. ul li {

76.    background-color: #FFFFFF;
```

```
77.      border: 1px solid #000000;

78.      list-style: none;

79.      margin: 1em 0;

80.      padding: 1em;

81. }

82. ul li.droppable-hover {

83.      background-color: #FFF000;

84. }

85. #category {

86.      border: 1px solid #000000;

87.      margin-top: 1em;

88.      padding: 1em;

89.      width: 97%;

90. }

91. #ui-draggable {

92.      background: #FF0000;

93.      padding: 1em;

94.      position: relative;

95.      width: 300px;

96. }

97. </style>

98. <h2><?php __('Categories');?></h2>
```

```
99.  <ul id="categories">

100.    <li id="category_0">

101.       <?php echo $this->element('draw_category', array('data' =>
        $categories)); ?>

102.    </li>

103.    <div id="category">

104.       <p>Enter a category name in the text box below, then drag the
        object below into the category you wish it to be a part of.</p>

105.       <div id="ui-draggable"><span></span></div>

106.       <?php echo $form->input('Category.name', array('onkeyup' =>
        'updateDragBox()')); ?>

107.    </div>

108. </ul>
```

The first thing we do is include our two jquery scripts. These can be downloaded from http://jquery.com and should be placed in the app\webroot\js folder.

The next thing we do is create Javascript code that is run when our document is finished loading. The first chunk of code creates our droppable elements. A droppable element is an element that can accept draggable elements. Each time a draggable element is released within it, an ondrop function is called that performs processing.

In our code, whenever an element is dropped on our droppable element, we need to update our tree. In our function, we retrieve some information through Javascript. Specifically the name of the category, the id of the droppable element (this will be the new parent id for the draggable element), and we also retrieve the id of the category being dropped. If it is new it will not have an id, if we are moving an existing one, we retrieve the id and perform an edit.

Once we have all of our data, we build two potential AJAX requests – one to add a new category and one to edit one. We then proceed to perform an AJAX post with the data. Once that AJAX request has completed, we perform a second AJAX request that will reload our category list with the new element in its appropriate position.

At the end of our onload function, we call another function that instantiates our draggable elements.

Our draggable elements consist of the same elements that are droppable because you may move a sub category (and its children) underneath or to a main category. One other element is defined as draggable as well. This element lives beneath our tree. As you type in the form, this element gets updated with the text entered. When you are satisfied with the name of your new category, you drag this element into the tree to insert it. The remaining Javascript functions deal with this.

After our Javascript is our CSS again. Normally this would go in a separate CSS file that we would include from our layout.

Next is our HTML code, as you may see, it's only 9 lines of code. The remaining code is in a recursive element that draws one level of categories at a time. In the app\views\elements directory, create a new file called draw_category.ctp. The contents of this file are below:

1. ```php
   <?php if ($data): ?><ul>
   ```

2. ```php
   <?php foreach ($data as $category): ?><li id="category_<?php echo $category['Category']['id']; ?>"><span><?php echo $category['Category']['name']; ?></span>
   ```

3. ```php
   <?php echo $this->element('draw_category', array('data' => $category['children'])); ?>
   ```

4. ```php
   </li><?php endforeach; ?>
   ```

5. ```php
   </ul><?php endif; ?>
   ```

In the index.ctp file, we pass our entire category tree to it. The element does a foreach statement through each category. Once we've displayed the main category, we call our element again passing in the children element.

SUMMARY

That completes today's lesson. Once you've saved your files you should be able to load http://localhost/HelloWorld/categories and see the dynamic category management system completely functional.

Below are a few screenshots of the process:
   ```

Figure 11: Initial View with no categories

Figure 12: Dragging a new category into the tree

Figure 13: Moving a sub category and its children

Challenge: Using what we learned when we setup our authentication, update the categories controller to ensure that we have a valid logged in user.

Figure 14: Multiple categories and sub categories

CHAPTER 9

ADDING SEO FUNCTIONALITY

Two of the biggest things that will improve your search engine rankings are keyword rich website titles and keyword rich links to your content. Today's lessons will cover both of these topics.

For more examples, visit the SEO category on my blog: http://www.endyourif.com/category/seo-search-engine-optimization/

OBJECTIVES

- Improve our search engine rankings

- Set a title tag

- Map a specific URL to a custom controller and action

- Avoid using ids or numbers in our URL

Before I start, I would like to make it clear that this chapter is and does not intend to be a be-all-to-end-all of the SEO necessities for your website. It is meant to describe some excellent techniques to quickly and easily improve upon CakePHP to make it more SEO friendly.

In this chapter we will focus on three techniques to easily adopt CakePHP and make it much more SEO friendly.

The three ways are:

- Use of title tags

- Use of routes

- Use of intelligent view() functions

USE OF TITLE TAGS

Let's begin with title tags. By default, if you do not set a title tag, CakePHP uses the name of your function. You will quickly find that this is not useful as Google frowns upon non-unique titles. Before long Google will have multiple title tags called Index and Add, etc... for your content. This will not get you too far.

CakePHP offers a simple solution to control this, you need to set a class variable called $pageTitle.

For example, inside anyone of our controllers we could do the following:

1. $this->pageTitle = 'This is our new title for this page!';

Obviously, this won't get you ranked very high either, but it may be better than Index!

USE OF ROUTES

Our next route is to use CakePHP routes, pun intended. Inside of the app\config directory there is a file called routes.php. Below is a default example of one:

1.   <?php

2.   /* SVN FILE: $Id: routes.php 7945 2008-12-19 02:16:01Z gwoo $ */

3.   /**

4.   Short description for file.

5.   *

6.   In this file, you set up routes to your controllers and their actions.

7.   Routes are very important mechanism that allows you to freely connect

8.   different urls to chosen controllers and their actions (functions).

9.   *

10. PHP versions 4 and 5

11. *

12. CakePHP(tm) : Rapid Development Framework
     (http://www.cakephp.org)

13. Copyright 2005-2008, Cake Software Foundation, Inc.
     (http://www.cakefoundation.org)

14. *

15. Licensed under The MIT License

16. Redistributions of files must retain the above copyright notice.

17. *

18. @filesource

19. * @copyright   Copyright 2005-2008, Cake Software Foundation,
     Inc. (http://www.cakefoundation.org)

20. * @link
     http://www.cakefoundation.org/projects/info/cakephp
     CakePHP(tm) Project

21. * @package   cake

22. * @subpackage   cake.app.config

23. * @since   CakePHP(tm) v 0.2.9

24. * @version $Revision: 7945 $

25. * @modifiedby $LastChangedBy: gwoo $

26. @lastmodified $Date: 2008-12-18 18:16:01 -0800 (Thu, 18 Dec 2008) $

27. * @license   http://www.opensource.org/licenses/mit-license.php The MIT License

28. */

29. /**

30. Here, we are connecting '/' (base path) to controller called 'Pages',

31. its action called 'display', and we pass a param to select the view file

32. to use (in this case, /app/views/pages/home.ctp)...

33. */

34. Router::connect('/', array('controller' => 'pages', 'action' => 'display', 'home'));

35. /**

36. ...and connect the rest of 'Pages' controller's urls.

37. */

38. Router::connect('/pages/*', array('controller' => 'pages', 'action' => 'display'));

```
39.  ?>
```

Ignoring all of the comments, the above file tells CakePHP that, when we arrive at "/", e.g. in our test project http://localhost/HelloWorld, that it should load the display() function in the pages_controller.php and pass in the variable "home". That means that it will load the home.ctp file inside our app\views\pages folder. If we don't create our own file with that name, CakePHP will load its default home.ctp file inside of cake\libs\view\pages.

The next action in the routes.php file tells CakePHP that any request to "/pages/*" should load this same display() function; however, instead of loading the home.ctp view, it will load whatever name we pass in. For example, if we visited http://localhost/HelloWorld/pages/test our CakePHP function would attempt to load app\views\pages\test.ctp and display it in our layout.

Now, how can we use routes to our advantage? Let's say we were to use CakePHP's bakery to create a user registration page. By default, we would access it as follows: http://localhost/HelloWorld/users/add. This is not the most user friendly URL in the world. Instead we want it to be: http://localhost/HelloWorld/register. To accomplish this, we would add the following line to our routes.php file:

```
1.  Router::connect('/register/*', array('controller' => 'users', 'action'
    => 'add'));
```

USE OF INTELLIGENT VIEW() FUNCTIONS

Our last example is to make intelligent view() functions. You may be wondering what I mean by an intelligent view function. Well, by default, when we use CakePHP's bakery all of our view functions load elements using   id's.   A   URL   like   this:

http://localhost/HelloWorld/categories/view/3 is not very search engine friendly. However, what if we could change this URL to: http://localhost/HelloWorld/categories/view/search-engine-optimization? This would certainly make it a lot better looking to search engines.

To accomplish this, we need to update our view function to have something similar to the following:

```
1.   function view($name = "") {

2.       // get the categories name and information

3.       if (intval($name) == 0 && strlen($name) == strlen(intval($name)))
         {

4.           $id = intval($name);

5.           $category = $this->Category->find('first', array('conditions' =>
         array('id' => $id)));

6.       } else {

7.           $category = $this->Category->find('first', array('conditions' =>
         array('name' => $name)));

8.       }

9.

10.      ...

11.

12.  }
```

In the above code, we check if name is an integer. If name is an integer, we will perform a regular search by id to get the record. However, if the name is actually a string, we will search for the category by name to find it. Technically we don't need to concern ourselves if an integer is passed into the function, but the first time I created a procedure like this, I already had indexed links with the id in the URL. Not wanting to lose these rankings, I made the function intelligent to handle both.

Challenge: Update a view() function to set the page title to name of our category that we are displaying. In the above example our page title should be: "Search Engine Optimization".

SUMMARY

As I mentioned at the beginning of this chapter, these three examples will considerably help your SEO rankings; however, don't stop there. If you are interested in SEO, perform some more research and see how you may utilize CakePHP to your advantage to quickly implement system-wide SEO changes.

CHAPTER 10

OPTIMIZING YOUR PROJECTS

CakePHP offers a lot of functionality to us as developers. The ability to develop websites rapidly provides a trade-off in how quickly the website will load. As we expand our skills, we will learn the techniques that will slow down/speed up performance.

For the complete source code, visit: http://www.endyourif.com/optimizing-cakephp-websites/

OBJECTIVES

- Apply techniques to speed up CakePHP's load time

- Optimize our queries

- Cache query results

Much like that last chapter on search engine optimization, improving your CakePHP projects is in no way an exact science.

There are many contributing factors that will help speed up certain aspects that may slow down others. In this chapter, I will cover various aspects of improvements that I've used successfully and explain how it improved our overall efficiency.

Hopefully the how will be the factor that is most clear. If you fully understand how different techniques help you will be able to pick the best methods for your project.

DEBUG MODE

I guess I may have lied; there is one thing that will work on *every* project and that is turning debugging off.

By default, when you setup a new CakePHP project the debug mode is set to 2. This is done inside of app\config\core.php with the following line:

1. Configure::write('debug', 2);

Debug mode of 2 means that CakePHP will display your database queries at the bottom of each page. It will also display all PHP errors and notices.

These errors and debug information are extremely important during development. However, when you are ready for production, be sure to *always* set it to 0.

By setting debug to 0, CakePHP will begin caching several elements of your project. By caching elements, your website is immediately sped up because CakePHP, for example, does not have to check the structure of each model on every page load.

> **TIP:** If you have successfully launched a website and set debug mode to 0, in the future when you add new controllers, or add new controller actions, or even change your database tables you will need to clear CakePHP's cache. My favorite solution is to temporarily change debug mode to 1, reload the website, and then set debug mode back to 0. This will ensure your new data is retrieved and once debug is back to 0, CakePHP will continue to cache your data.

RECURSIVE FIND STATEMENTS

You may notice that when we use the bakery, our index function has the following line of code prior to performing the pagination find statement:

```
1.  $this->Model->recursive = 0;
```

The following line tells CakePHP to join our tables related to this model. For example, in our albums controller, when we perform the find statement, not only will it retrieve all of our albums, it will also return all of the photos for each album.

In several instances this certainly is desired. However, it is important to analyze each query individually to ensure we have the correct recursive level setting.

To ensure that we only query the one model and do not perform any join statements, use the following setting for recursion:

```
1.  $this->Model->recursive = -1;
```

REQUESTACTION AVOIDANCE

This is a tough one that I still struggle with on a daily basis. A request action allows you to call other controller functions inside another view or controller. This makes re-using code extremely beneficial during development. However, each time you do a request action, CakePHP goes through the entire dispatch process.

At this point, I have yet to find a satisfactory alternative to this and each time I make a different decision; other times I continue to use requestActions because I determine it will not hurt my load time in that instance.

My rule of thumb is as follows, if I can alter the code, split it up more and avoid request actions without too much duplicated code or complications, I will do that.   If it's relatively difficult and time consuming, I will take the hit and use a requestAction() call.

A solution that has worked well for me is to place the views HTML code in an element. Then instead of using a requestAction I load an element() from the two views. This will not work 100% yet, more work is required. We also need to be sure to include the code in the controller from our other function.

To accomplish this, I will move and re-organize the code around. If it works, this is a great place to create components; if that doesn't work, creating private functions in your controllers will work as well.

CACHING QUERY RESULTS

By default, most database servers will cache our database queries for us; however, regardless if the server caches your query, CakePHP still needs to perform the action and parse the results and build us our useful arrays of data.

By caching our query results with CakePHP, we can avoid all of this processing. Time savings here can be incredible based on the data being cached and processed.

Over time, I have built an excellent process that allows me to cache any query results I wish using CakePHP's built-in caching system.

Before we begin, I need to post a big disclaimer...BE VERY CAREFUL WITH WHAT DATA YOU CACHE! As Peter Parker's Uncle Sam once told him, "With great power, comes great responsibility". The same applies here. Caching your data can be extremely useful, but it can be very bad if you cache data incorrectly. You will begin seeing incorrect data appear, errors because the data is not what was expected, the list could go on and on.

Don't be scared though, we just need to use it correctly and we will have great success!

Step 1, create an app_model.php. This file should live in the root of your "app" folder. Below is an example of my app_model.php, it contains one function called find().

```
1.   class AppModel extends Model {

2.

3.      function find($conditions = null, $fields = array(), $order = null,
        $recursive = null) {

4.          $doQuery = true;

5.          // check if we want the cache

6.          if (!empty($fields['cache'])) {

7.              $cacheConfig = null;

8.              // check if we have specified a custom config, e.g. different
        expiry time

9.              if (!empty($fields['cacheConfig']))

10.                 $cacheConfig = $fields['cacheConfig'];

11.                 $cacheName = $this->name . '-' . $fields['cache'];
```

```
12.

13.                  // if so, check if the cache exists

14.                  if (($data = Cache::read($cacheName, $cacheConfig))
        === false) {

15.                      $data = parent::find($conditions, $fields, $order,
        $recursive);

16.                      Cache::write($cacheName, $data, $cacheConfig);

17.                  }

18.                  $doQuery = false;

19.              }

20.              if ($doQuery)

21.                  $data = parent::find($conditions, $fields, $order,
        $recursive);

22.

23.          return $data;

24.      }

25.

26. }
```

The following code overrides the find() function in the main model class. It looks for an array key called "cache". This is a new key that we are implementing. If this key is found, we generate our cache name. It's the modelName-cacheName. We automatically append the model name to help prevent cross-table contamination incase we accidently used the same name twice!

We also look for another new key called cacheConfig. If this exists, it allows us to specify a different timeout period for our cached data. By default, it uses CakePHP's default caching. I'm not exactly sure what it is, I think it's in the one week range.

We then proceed to read the cache with that name. If it does not exist, we execute the query and save the results to the cache for next time.

If we wished to cache data for a shorter (or longer) period of time, we would create a new config item in our app/config/core.php file as shown here:

```
1.   Cache::config('short', array(

2.        'engine' => 'File',

3.        'duration'=> '+5 minutes',

4.        'probability'=> 100,

5.        'path' => CACHE . 'short' . DS,

6.   ));
```

The following code creates a config setting named "short". We tell it to only cache our data for 5 minutes. This is great for something on the homepage that we don't want to reload every time, but don't want it to be cached for a long time either.

While we are in our app/config/core.php, it's a good idea to ensure the following line is uncommented:

```
1.   Configure::write('Cache.check', true);
```

Ok, now we have everything setup to use, so how do we use it? Good question, let's pretend we have a lookup table for a list of countries. It's pretty safe to assume that we will not be changing the data fairly often, so we should cache the query results. To accomplish this, we do the following (this assumes we have a "Country" model and a "Countries" controller)

```
1.   // get country list using default config

2.   $countries = $this->Country->find('list', array('cache' =>
     'countryList'));

3.

4.   // get country list using a custom config

5.   $countries = $this->Country->find('list', array('cache' =>
     'countryList', 'cacheConfig' => 'long'));
```

The following code executes a straight forward find statement. The first time it runs, CakePHP will execute the find query, parse the results, and save the data to the cache. The next time though, it will find the cached results and return those to us without the need to perform a database query and process the results.

To take this one extra step and make it even more useful, assuming we have a countries_controller.php file that allows us to add, edit, and delete countries. We can update these three functions to remove our cached data. This way, next time the countries are queried, it will not load the stale data; it will load the fresh data.

To accomplish this add the following line inside add, edit, and delete functions. I would place it inside the if ($this->Country->save(…)) statement so we only do it on a successful action:

```
1.   // we need to remove the status cache now

2.   Cache::delete('Country-countryList');
```

It's important to note that I did NOT just use countryList like in the find statement. Instead, I prefixed the model name "Country" and a hyphen as well.

That's all there is to it. For a good starting place, I would cache all of your "lookup" table queries, similar to the country list above. From there, I'll let your imagination do the trick. One piece of advice though, if you are caching a query that contains a "where id = $logged_in_user" (or any other conditional statements), be sure you include the $logged_in_user in the name of the "cache" key; otherwise, you will load the wrong person's data!

SUMMARY

The above methods are my favorite ways of optimizing CakePHP. At this point, it's a good idea to remember not to assume *all* speed issues are caused by the framework. It is still to important to confirm that we've ruled out other issues. For example:

- Poor database indexes

- Poor database queries

- Too many database queries

- Too many Javascript files

- Too many CSS files

- Etc, Etc, Etc...

If you think one of the issues above may be the cause, I would like to refer you to an excellent blog article I wrote a while ago: http://www.endyourif.com/yslow-helping-slow-web-pages-load-faster/

The article is called "YSlow – Helping Slow Web Pages Load Faster". It provides some excellent techniques to improve any website, not just CakePHP specific websites.

CHAPTER 11

PUTTING IT ALL TOGETHER

You are almost a CakePHP expert. This final chapter will teach you how to tie all of our individual chapters together to form a complete project. To ensure we succeed, we will define a process that will take us step-by-step through the development life cycle.

OBJECTIVES

- Understand how to complete a project from start-to-finish

- Create a content management system

- Submit comments through AJAX

- Combine our previous code into a complete project

Congratulations, you've made it this far! I hope by this point you are relatively comfortable with many aspects of CakePHP. To wrap it up, let's build a final project that will be useful, teach us something, and finally, make us proud.

In this final chapter, we will attempt to use all of our CakePHP knowledge and bring it all together. So, what should we build? While writing the book I struggled with this one for a little bit. After some thinking, it became quite clear to me. What is one of the most popular things on the Internet today? The answer to this is blogs and blogging software. The other question that came to mind is what do I build at work more frequently than anything else? The answer to that question is: Content Management System, also known as, CMS.

When you think about it, a blog is a CMS because using your favorite blogging software; you are first and foremost just managing content. I thought building a CMS would both be fun and useful. In case you think this may be boring or not interesting, don't worry, I plan to add several elements that will be both fun and a good learning experience.

By the end of this chapter we will have a fully functional CMS that we can manage our content easily and categorize it using our category management. Each time a page is saved, we will create a revision history that will allow changes to be reverted. Front-end users will be able to view the content, register as a new user, and post comments dynamically using AJAX.

Figure 15: Add new page

Without further ado, let's begin.

In our previous chapters, we only ever had a few small goals; with this final project we have quite a few goals. Let's spend a few minutes discussing how to undertake a large task like this.

Below is my standard approach to a new project:

- Determine scope of work

- Create database schema

- Import database

- Use the bakery to create our models, controllers, and views

- Main development

- Testing

- Finishing touches

- Go live

This is an excellent high level to do list. Let's start with the first one.

DETERMINE SCOPE OF WORK

The scope of work will be our guideline throughout the remainder of our project. Our first draft is usually relatively accurate; however, as most projects move along, the scope moves with it. Reasons can vary from difficulties with a perceived approach; new functionality wanted; a change in direction, etc... No matter the reason, it's important to keep the scope up-to-date. This is our checklist to ensure we've accomplished all pieces of the project.

Here is my rough draft for this project:

1. **Create database**

   1.1. Optimize database by adding indexes for improved query performance

2. **Design**

   2.1. Create basic design to allow us to navigate through the site

3. **Homepage**

   3.1. Create a listing of pages. Include a link to view the full detail as well as a link to view the comments with a count of how many there are

4. **Category Listing**

   4.1. List categories on the left-hand side. When a category is selected, filter the pages for that category

5. **Registration**

   5.1. Create a page that allows a user to register and submit comments

6. **Login**

    6.1. Create a form to collect login information

    6.2. On submission, process login and setup session variables

7. **Logout**

    7.1. Upon logout, clear out all session data

8. **Page Display**

    8.1. After a link from the homepage has been clicked, display the full details of the page

    8.2. List the comments for this page

9. **Add Comments**

    9.1. At the bottom of each page, include a form to add comments. Comments will be submitted and added through AJAX

10. **Admin Area**

    10.1. If the user is an admin, display extra navigation for admin controls

11. **Page Management**

    11.1. List pages

11.1.1. Include a link to view revisions of previous versions

11.1.2. List revisions

11.1.3. Revert to previous revision

11.2. Add page

11.2.1. Include fckEditor to allow creation of HTML pages

11.3. Edit page

11.3.1. Prior to saving, create a revision of the page

11.4. Delete page

11.4.1. Upon deletion, delete all revision history of this page

12. Category Management

12.1. List categories and its subcategories

12.2. Add (sub)category

12.3. Move (sub)category

This completes our scope of work. It's important to provide a decent amount of details in the descriptions above. This will ensure nothing important is missed during the development process.

DATABASE CONFIGURATION

Before we create our actual database on the server, I like to create a visual representation of what it will look like.

During this stage, I'm not overly concerned about perfecting each table. I normally have a good idea of what each table will look like, so I'll attempt to capture as much as I can knowing I may miss a few fields here and there.

My main focus is to ensure that I have all tables thought about and how each table is related to each other.

To create my schema, there are several useful tools that exist:

- Mysql Workbench – Free from mysql.com

- PHPMyAdmin – Free from phpmyadmin.net. Here you need to use the designer

- Microsoft Visio – Expensive from Microsoft

- Microsoft Access – Included with Microsoft Office

- Microsoft SQL Server – Expensive database server. Here you need to use the designer

- Draw it by hand – If I'm in a hurry, this is an excellent, cheap solution

My personal favorite is Microsoft Visio, but I only have access to this at work. For my personal projects I choose Mysql Workbench.

For this project our lists of tables are: users, categories, pages, pages_revisions, and pages_comments.

Once we've created our tables, we need to create the relationships. Categories are related to pages; pages are related to revisions; pages are related to comments; and finally, users are related to comments.

We now should have a very clear picture of what our database will look like.

IMPORT DATABASE

With our schema created, most of the above programs offer a way to export the database. Use the help feature of the associated program and do this now.

Below is a sample listing of our completed tables:

1. CREATE TABLE `categories` (

2. `id` int(10) unsigned NOT NULL auto_increment,

3. `name` varchar(255) NOT NULL,

4. `parent_id` int(10) unsigned NOT NULL,

5. `page_count` int(10) unsigned NOT NULL,

6. `lft` int(10) unsigned NOT NULL,

7. `rght` int(10) unsigned NOT NULL,

8.   PRIMARY KEY (`id`)

9.   ) ENGINE=InnoDB DEFAULT CHARSET=latin1;

10.

11. CREATE TABLE `pages` (

12.   `id` int(10) unsigned NOT NULL auto_increment,

13.   `pages_comment_count` int(10) unsigned NOT NULL,

14.   `title` varchar(255) NOT NULL,

15.   `body` text NOT NULL,

16.   `category_id` int(10) unsigned NOT NULL,

17.   `created` datetime default NULL,

18.   `modified` datetime default NULL,

19.   PRIMARY KEY (`id`)

20.) ENGINE=InnoDB DEFAULT CHARSET=latin1;

21.

22. CREATE TABLE `pages_comments` (

23.   `id` int(10) unsigned NOT NULL auto_increment,

24.   `page_id` int(10) unsigned NOT NULL,

25.   `user_id` int(10) unsigned NOT NULL,

26.   `comment` text NOT NULL,

27.   `created` datetime default NULL,

28.   `modified` datetime default NULL,

29.   PRIMARY KEY (`id`)

```
30.  ) ENGINE=InnoDB DEFAULT CHARSET=latin1;

31.

32.  CREATE TABLE `pages_revisions` (

33.      `id` int(10) unsigned NOT NULL auto_increment,

34.      `page_id` int(10) unsigned NOT NULL,

35.      `title` varchar(255) NOT NULL,

36.      `body` text NOT NULL,

37.      `category_id` int(10) unsigned NOT NULL,

38.      `created` datetime default NULL,

39.      `modified` datetime default NULL,

40.      PRIMARY KEY (`id`)

41.  ) ENGINE=InnoDB DEFAULT CHARSET=latin1;

42.

43.  CREATE TABLE `users` (

44.      `id` int(10) unsigned NOT NULL auto_increment,

45.      `first_name` varchar(45) NOT NULL,

46.      `last_name` varchar(45) NOT NULL,

47.      `email` varchar(150) NOT NULL,

48.      `password` varchar(45) NOT NULL,

49.      `address` varchar(45) default NULL,

50.      `address2` varchar(45) default NULL,

51.      `city` varchar(45) default NULL,
```

52. `state` varchar(45) default NULL,

53. `zipcode` varchar(10) default NULL,

54. `country` varchar(45) default NULL,

55. `is_admin` tinyint(3) unsigned NOT NULL,

56. `created` datetime default NULL,

57. `modified` datetime default NULL,

58. PRIMARY KEY (`id`)

59.) ENGINE=InnoDB DEFAULT CHARSET=latin1;

You may notice that most of the create statements are from previous chapters. The new ones are all related to our pages for our CMS.

USING THE BAKERY

Now that we have our database created, we can create our core code. Rather than typing it ourselves, let's go back to "Chapter 4: How to use the bakery" and have CakePHP create the code for us.

Let's start by creating all of our models. Nothing special should be required and most, if not all, of the defaults should get us through the process.

Next we need to create our controllers. We'll bake all of our controllers; none of them need admin routing. Once we get to the main development, we'll make the necessary changes to accomplish all of the functionality required.

Once we've created both our models and controllers, we can finish by creating our views. We'll need views for all of the controllers. We don't need any admin routes.

That's it for the easy parts. Now it's time to get down and dirty and perform our actual development. Thankfully, CakePHP has taken care of a large portion of it; our job won't be difficult at all!

MAIN DEVELOPMENT

Before we start our main development, I would like to describe a bit about my development strategy. I'm not one of those people that can focus on one task at a time, especially at the start of a project.

After I've baked the core of my files, I begin scattering all over the place taking care of small things. For example, I would create an app_controller.php, setup authentication. I would then jump immediately to the users_controller.php and create my login and logout functions. Then I would jump ship and create the views for the login.

At this point the login process would be finished. I would next jump to creating some basic navigation to maneuver around the site. Once I've gotten this far, I can then proceed to accomplishing the bigger tasks.

Throughout the entire process, I don't even bother opening a web browser to see how it looks. I'm fairly confident in my typing skills and my CakePHP skills that I just whip through the coding.

After a little while, I'll stop and begin testing and marking items off that I've completed. In our A.D.D (Attention Deficit Disorder) society, I find this quite effective and I can accomplish things 10 times faster than I normally would.

This approach may not work for everyone. However, I would strive yourself to get to this goal because you will really begin to see how quickly your development time will begin to drop. The important part to remember is, don't get frustrated when you begin testing and you have a lot of little errors. I normally find myself making it 90% of the way and I just have to fix a few things which don't take very long at all.

Unfortunately, for the purpose of this book, it would be very impractical and difficult to follow such an approach. Instead I've done this in advance and will provide a more structured approach.

Let's begin by setting up our app_controller. Using the lessons we learned in "Chapter 5: How to setup Authentication", we'll create our app controller and initialize the authentication portion.

```php
1.   <?php

2.   class AppController extends Controller {

3.      var $components = array('Auth');

4.

5.      function beforeFilter() {

6.         $this->Auth->userModel = 'User';

7.         $this->Auth->authorize = 'controller';

8.         $this->Auth->fields = array('username' => 'email', 'password'
         => 'password');

9.         $this->Auth->loginAction = array('admin' => false, 'controller'
         => 'users', 'action' => 'login');

10.        $this->Auth->loginRedirect = array('/');
```

```
11.

12.        if ($this->Auth->user()) {

13.            $this->set('user_id', $this->Auth->user('id'));

14.            $this->set('is_admin', $this->Auth->user('is_admin'));

15.        }

16.    }

17.

18. }

19. ?>
```

In the above code, we create a beforeFilter() function. This function will be called on each page load by the controller. It initiates our authentication and sets a few parameters telling CakePHP how it should authenticate our users.

The last few lines of this function set a couple parameters for our views. If the user is logged in, we want to pass the user_id to our views as well as if the user is an admin user. These will be used later by our default layout.

Next, will be our users_controller.php. After we've baked the users_controller.php, we will remove several functions that will not be part of this process and add several more. Below is a completed version of our controller:

```php
1.    <?php

2.    class UsersController extends AppController {

3.        var $name = 'Users';

4.        var $helpers = array('Html', 'Form');

5.

6.        function beforeFilter() {

7.            parent::beforeFilter();

8.            // allow everything

9.            $this->Auth->allow('*');

10.       }

11.

12.       function add() {

13.           if (!empty($this->data)) {

14.               $this->User->create();

15.               if ($this->User->save($this->data)) {

16.                   $this->Session->setFlash('User successfully created');

17.                   $this->redirect('/');

18.               } else {

19.                   $this->Session->setFlash('There was an error saving the
      user');
```

```
20.          }

21.        }

22.      }

23.

24.    /**

25.    The AuthComponent provides the needed functionality

26.    for login, so you can leave this function blank.

27.    */

28.    function login() {}

29.

30.    function logout() {

31.        $this->redirect($this->Auth->logout());

32.    }

33.  }

34. ?>
```

The first function in the above code is another beforeFilter() function. Because each controller requires different authentication permissions, all of our controllers will contain this function. In the case of our user's controller, we allow access to everything. Apart from that, this controller is exactly the same as back in Chapter 5.

To keep things moving without the need to jump around, we'll continue describing our remaining controllers.

Below is our categories_controller.php:

```php
1.  <?php
2.  class CategoriesController extends AppController {
3.      var $name = 'Categories';
4.      var $helpers = array('Html', 'Form', 'Javascript');
5.      var $components = array('RequestHandler');
6.
7.      function beforeFilter() {
8.          parent::beforeFilter();
9.          $this->Auth->deny('index', 'add', 'delete');
10.         if ($this->Auth->user('is_admin'))
11.             $this->Auth->allow('*');
12.         else
13.             $this->Auth->allow('public_list');
14.     }
15.
16.     function index() {
17.         // if it's ajax, set ajax layout
18.         if ($this->RequestHandler->isAjax())
19.             $this->layout = 'ajax';
20.         $categories = $this->Category->find('threaded');
21.         $this->set(compact('categories'));
```

```
22.    }

23.

24.    function public_list() {

25.        $categories = $this->Category->find('threaded');

26.        $this->set(compact('categories'));

27.        $this->render();

28.    }

29.

30.    function add() {

31.        if (!empty($this->data)) {

32.            $this->Category->create();

33.            if ($this->Category->save($this->data)) {

34.                $this->Session->setFlash(__('The Category has been
       saved', true));

35.                //$this->redirect(array('action'=>'index'));

36.            } else {

37.                $this->Session->setFlash(__('The Category could not be
       saved. Please, try again.', true));

38.            }

39.        }

40.        $this->render(false);

41.    }

42.
```

```php
43.    function edit($id = null) {

44.        if (!$id && empty($this->data)) {

45.            $this->Session->setFlash(__('Invalid Category', true));

46.            $this->redirect(array('action'=>'index'));

47.        }

48.        if (!empty($this->data)) {

49.            if ($this->Category->save($this->data)) {

50.                $this->Session->setFlash(__('The Category has been saved', true));

51.                //$this->redirect(array('action'=>'index'));

52.            } else {

53.                $this->Session->setFlash(__('The Category could not be saved. Please, try again.', true));

54.            }

55.        }

56.        if (empty($this->data)) {

57.            $this->data = $this->Category->read(null, $id);

58.        }

59.        $this->render(false);

60.    }

61.

62.    function delete($id = null) {

63.        if (!$id) {
```

```
64.          $this->Session->setFlash(__('Invalid id for Category', true));

65.          $this->redirect(array('action'=>'index'));

66.     }

67.     if ($this->Category->del($id)) {

68.          $this->Session->setFlash(__('Category deleted', true));

69.          $this->redirect(array('action'=>'index'));

70.     }

71.   }

72. }

73. ?>
```

Our categories controller is very similar to the one we created in "Chapter 8: Act like a tree" with a few small additions. The first one is our beforeFilter() function. By default we deny the index, add, edit, and delete functions. If the user is an admin, they are allowed access to everything; otherwise, only the public_listing() function should be available.

The public_listing() function is our other new function. This will be used on the homepage to display a list of categories on the left-hand side.

The next controller is a new one that has more custom code, it is our pages_controller.php:

```
1.   <?php

2.   class PagesController extends AppController {

3.     var $name = 'Pages';
```

```
4.      var $helpers = array('Html', 'Form', 'Javascript');

5.      var $components = array('File');

6.

7.      function beforeFilter() {

8.          parent::beforeFilter();

9.          // allow everything for admin

10.         if ($this->Auth->user('is_admin') == 1)

11.             $this->Auth->allow('*');

12.         else

13.             $this->Auth->allow('home', 'display');

14.     }

15.

16.     function home($category = null) {

17.         $conditions = array();

18.         if ($category) {

19.             // find the category by name

20.             $this->Page->Category->recursive = -1;

21.             $category = $this->Page->Category->find('first',
        array('fields' => 'id', 'conditions' => array('name' => $category)));

22.             // did we find the category?

23.             if ($category)

24.                 $conditions = array('category_id' =>
        $category['Category']['id']);
```

```
25.    }

26.    // get the list of pages, if a category is passed in, filter by that

27.    $this->Page->recursive = -1;

28.    $pages = $this->Page->find('all', array('conditions' =>
       $conditions));

29.    $this->set('pages', $pages);

30.    // pass the file component to the function so we can call our
       function to clean the title

31.    $this->set('file', $this->File);

32.    }

33.

34.    function index() {

35.        $this->Page->recursive = 0;

36.        $this->set('pages', $this->paginate());

37.    }

38.

39.    function add() {

40.        if (!empty($this->data)) {

41.            $this->Page->create();

42.            if ($this->Page->save($this->data)) {

43.                // save a physical copy of the file

44.                $this->data['Page']['id'] = $this->Page->id;

45.                $this->File->saveFile($this->data);
```

```
46.            $this->Session->setFlash(__('The Page has been saved',
        true));

47.            $this->redirect(array('action'=>'index'));

48.        } else {

49.            $this->Session->setFlash(__('The Page could not be
        saved. Please, try again.', true));

50.        }

51.    }

52.    $categories = $this->Page->Category->find('list');

53.    $this->set(compact('categories'));

54.    }

55.

56.    function edit($id = null) {

57.        if (!$id && empty($this->data)) {

58.            $this->Session->setFlash(__('Invalid Page', true));

59.            $this->redirect(array('action'=>'index'));

60.        }

61.        if (!empty($this->data)) {

62.            if ($this->Page->save($this->data)) {

63.                // save a physical copy of the file

64.                $this->File->saveFile($this->data);

65.                $this->Session->setFlash(__('The Page has been saved',
        true));
```

```
66.              $this->redirect(array('action'=>'index'));

67.          } else {

68.              $this->Session->setFlash(__('The Page could not be
         saved. Please, try again.', true));

69.          }

70.      }

71.      if (empty($this->data)) {

72.          $this->data = $this->Page->read(null, $id);

73.      }

74.      $categories = $this->Page->Category->find('list');

75.      $this->set(compact('categories'));

76.  }

77.

78.  function delete($id = null) {

79.      if (!$id) {

80.          $this->Session->setFlash(__('Invalid id for Page', true));

81.          $this->redirect(array('action'=>'index'));

82.      }

83.      // get our file name

84.      $this->Page->id = $id;

85.      $page = $this->Page->read();

86.      if ($this->Page->del($id)) {
```

```
87.         // delete our file

88.         $this->File->deleteFile($page);

89.         $this->Session->setFlash(__('Page deleted', true));

90.         $this->redirect(array('action'=>'index'));

91.     }

92.  }

93.

94.  /**

95.  Displays a view

96.  *

97.  @param mixed What page to display

98.  @access public

99.  */

100. function display() {

101.    $path = func_get_args();

102.    $count = count($path);

103.    if (!$count) {

104.        $this->redirect('/');

105.    }

106.    $page = $subpage = $title = null;

107.    if (!empty($path[0])) {

108.        $page = $path[0];
```

```
109.      }

110.      if (!empty($path[1])) {

111.          $subpage = $path[1];

112.      }

113.      if (!empty($path[$count - 1])) {

114.          $title = Inflector::humanize($path[$count - 1]);

115.      }

116.      $this->set(compact('page', 'subpage', 'title'));

117.      $this->render(join('/', $path));

118.  }

119. }

120. ?>
```

Like our categories controller, the beforeFilter() function acts in the same way. The only difference is we have two public functions that are allowed by non-admin users (home and display).

The next function is our home() function. This will be our default function when we first visit the website. It accepts one optional parameter. If a category is passed into the function, we find the id of the category by its name. This process is similar to "Chapter 9: Adding SEO functionality". We then proceed to find a list of pages and filter by the optional category id.

The next four functions: index(), add(), edit(), and delete() are the functions that are completed by the bakery. We've made slight editions to each of the functions. It will either save a physical copy of the file or remove the physical copy from the hard drive.

You may notice several calls to "$this->File". We've created a component called "FileComponent" that handles our file manipulation. We'll discuss this in more detail shortly.

The last function in our controller is the display() function. This function is the default CakePHP function that loads our static pages views. The function was copied from cake\libs\controller\pages_controller.php.

The next controller is our pages_comments_controller.php.

```php
1.   <?php

2.   class PagesCommentsController extends AppController {

3.       var $name = 'PagesComments';

4.       var $helpers = array('Html', 'Form', 'Ajax');

5.       var $components = array('RequestHandler');

6.

7.       function beforeFilter() {

8.           parent::beforeFilter();

9.           // allow index for all

10.          $this->Auth->allow('*');

11.          if (!$this->Auth->user())

12.              $this->Auth->deny('add', 'delete');

13.      }

14.

15.      function index($page_id = null) {
```

```
16.        if (!$page_id) {

17.            $this->Session->setFlash(__('Invalid PagesComment', true));

18.            $this->redirect(array('controller' => 'pages',
           'action'=>'home'));

19.        }

20.        $this->set('page_id', $page_id);

21.        $this->PagesComment->recursive = 0;

22.        $this->set('pagesComments', $this-
           >paginate('PagesComment', array('page_id' => intval($page_id))));

23.        $this->render();

24.    }

25.

26.    function add($page_id = null) {

27.        if (!$page_id && empty($this->data)) {

28.            $this->Session->setFlash(__('Invalid PagesComment', true));

29.        }

30.        if (!empty($this->data)) {

31.            $this->data['PagesComment']['user_id'] = $this->Auth-
           >user('id');

32.            $this->PagesComment->create();

33.            if ($this->PagesComment->save($this->data)) {

34.                $this->Session->setFlash(__('The PagesComment has
           been saved', true));

35.            } else {
```

```
36.                $this->Session->setFlash(__('The PagesComment could
      not be saved. Please, try again.', true));

37.          }

38.        } else {

39.            $this->data['PagesComment']['page_id'] = $page_id;

40.        }

41.    }

42.

43.    function delete($id = null, $page_id = null) {

44.        if (!$id || !$page_id) {

45.            $this->Session->setFlash(__('Invalid id for PagesComment',
      true));

46.        }

47.        if ($this->PagesComment->del($id)) {

48.            $this->Session->setFlash(__('PagesComment deleted',
      true));

49.        }

50.    }

51. }

52. ?>
```

Apart from the beforeFilter() function, this controller is from the bakery. The edit() and view() function have been removed because they are not needed. This controller allows users to comment on a specific page. Our before filter allows the index page to all, but denies the add and delete functions if the user is not logged in.

Our last controller is the pages_revisions_controller.php. This controller displays a list of revisions for a specific page. A page can be reverted back to a previous version through this controller.

```php
1.  <?php

2.  class PagesRevisionsController extends AppController {

3.      var $name = 'PagesRevisions';

4.      var $helpers = array('Html', 'Form');

5.

6.      function beforeFilter() {

7.          parent::beforeFilter();

8.          $this->Auth->deny('index', 'view', 'revert');

9.          if ($this->Auth->user('is_admin'))

10.             $this->Auth->allow('*');

11.     }

12.

13.     function index($page_id = null) {

14.         if (!$page_id) {

15.             $this->Session->setFlash(__('Invalid Page.', true));

16.             $this->redirect(array('controller' => 'pages', 'action'=>'index'));

17.         }
```

```
18.        $this->PagesRevision->recursive = 0;

19.        $this->paginate['conditions']['page_id'] = $page_id;

20.        $this->set('pagesRevisions', $this->paginate());

21.    }

22.

23.    function view($id = null, $page_id = null) {

24.        if (!$id || !$page_id) {

25.            $this->Session->setFlash(__('Invalid PagesRevision.', true));

26.            $this->redirect(array('action'=>'index'));

27.        }

28.        $this->set('page_id', $page_id);

29.        $this->PagesRevision->recursive = 0;

30.        $this->set('pagesRevision', $this->PagesRevision->read(null,
       $id));

31.    }

32.

33.    function revert($id = null) {

34.        if (!$id) {

35.            $this->Session->setFlash(__('Invalid Page.', true));

36.            $this->redirect(array('controller' => 'pages',
       'action'=>'index'));
```

```
37.        }

38.        $this->PagesRevision->revertPage($id);

39.        $this->Session->setFlash(__('The page has been successfully
    reverted', true));

40.        $this->redirect(array('controller' => 'pages', 'action'=>'index'));

41.    }

42.  }

43.  ?>
```

This controller is 100% admin only. Our beforeFilter() function denies everything unless the user is an admin.

The index() and view() functions are from the bakery. We've removed the add(), edit(), and delete() functions. The last function is our revert() function. This calls a function in our model that performs the necessary work to revert the page. This function will be discussed in more detail when we describe our models.

Figure 16: Page revision view

During the testing process of this code, as well from past experiences, I've come to notice a bug in the AuthComponent provided with CakePHP. At the time of writing, this issue has *not* been resolved yet. The issue is in our add form.   It does not properly handle blank passwords. Rather than displaying an error message from the validation, the blank password is MD5 encrypted causing the validation to be skipped.

The fix to this is quite simple.   Begin by copying this file: cake\libs\controller\components\auth.php   to app\controllers\components\auth.php. Once the file has been copied, open the newly copied file.

The following line:

```
1.   if (isset($data[$this->userModel][$this->fields['username']])) &&
```

```
isset($data[$this->userModel][$this->fields['password']]])) {
```

Becomes:

1. if (isset($data[$this->userModel][$this->fields['username']]]) &&
    !empty($data[$this->userModel][$this->fields['password']]])) {

The change is we want to use !empty() around the password field opposed to the isset() function. This line is approximately around 845.

While we are in the components directory, let's describe our aforementioned FileComponent. Create a new file called file.php:

1.  ```php
    <?php
    ```

2. class FileComponent extends Object {

3.

4.   function saveFile($data) {

5.   // append our comments request action

6. $data['Page']['body'] .= "\n" . '<!--- ADD COMMENTS TO PAGE --->';

7. $data['Page']['body'] .= "\n" . '<?php echo $this->requestAction("/pages_comments/index/' . $data['Page']['id'] . '");?>';

8.   // clean the file name and replace spaces with dashes

9.   // and save the file locally

10.   file_put_contents($this->buildPath($data), $data['Page']['body']);
    ```

```
11.    }

12.

13.    function deleteFile($data) {

14.        // clean the file name and replace spaces with dashes

15.        // and delete the file locally

16.        if (file_exists($filepath = $this->buildPath($data))) {

17.            unlink($filepath);

18.        }

19.    }

20.

21.    function buildPath($data, $full = true) {

22.        App::import('Sanitize');

23.        if ($full)

24.            return APP . 'views\\pages\\' .
       Sanitize::paranoid(str_replace(' ', '-', $data['Page']['title']), array('-'))
       . '.ctp';

25.        else

26.            return Sanitize::paranoid(str_replace(' ', '-',
       $data['Page']['title']), array('-'));

27.    }

28.
```

```
29.      function unbuildPath($data) {

30.          return str_replace('-', ' ', $data);

31.      }

32. }

33. ?>
```

The following component has four functions.   The first function saveFile() receives our data from the add and edit form of the pages controller.   We append a requestAction() to the body.   This requestAction() will display our comments for that page. We proceed to write the file to the hard drive. We use our buildPath() function to set the location of where the file will be written to.

The buildPath() function removes non-alphanumeric characters from it and replaces all spaces with hyphens.

The deleteFile() function also uses this function and checks to see if the file exists. If it does exist, we remove the file from the hard drive.

The last function performs the opposite of build path in that it replaces hyphens with spaces.

The brains of our code are now mostly completed. Let's move on and begin discussing the models. For the most part our models are quite bare; however, a few of them have some important functions in them.

Our first model is the category model. The only change to this model from the bakery is the following line:

1.   var $actsAs = array('Tree');

This can be placed after the name variable. For more information on this behavior, review "Chapter 8: Act like a tree".

Our next model is the page model. This model uses several callback methods. A callback method is a function that is called before and after specific actions. For example, beforeFind() and afterFind() are called before and after every find statement.

Our page model uses these callback functions to maintain our revision history. The two callback functions are below:

```
1.    function beforeSave() {

2.        // only create revision if id is > 0

3.        if (!empty($this->data['Page']['id'])) {

4.            // import our PagesRevision model

5.            App::import('model', 'PagesRevision');

6.            // instantiate it

7.            $this->PagesRevision = new PagesRevision();

8.            $this->PagesRevision->saveRevision($this->data);

9.        }

10.       return true;

11.   }

12.
```

```
13.  function afterDelete() {

14.      // import our PagesRevision model

15.      App::import('model', 'PagesRevision');

16.      // instantiate it

17.      $this->PagesRevision = new PagesRevision();

18.      $this->PagesRevision->deleteRevision($this->data['Page']['id']);

19.  }
```

The first function, beforeSave(), checks if the page is new or if we are editing. If we are editing, the id for the page will not be empty. In this case we import our PagesRevision model and call our custom function saveRevision(). This function will be described shortly.

The second function, afterDelete(), removes the entire revision history for that page. Like the previous function, it also instantiates the PagesRevision model and calls a custom function in that model to perform the deletion.

The last thing we need to do to this model is update the "belongsTo" category array. CakePHP offers a nice feature called "counterCache". Each time we insert and delete data, if we have a field called page_count in our categories table, CakePHP will automatically update this number for us. We'll use this field later to display how many pages are in the category.

```
1.   var $belongsTo = array(

2.      'Category' => array('className' => 'Category',

3.            'foreignKey' => 'category_id',

4.            'conditions' => '',

5.            'fields' => '',

6.            'order' => '',

7.            'counterCache' => true

8.      )

9.   );
```

Our next model is the pages revision model. This model contains three custom functions that we've briefly touched upon earlier.

```
1.   function saveRevision($data) {

2.      // get our current page

3.      $this->Page->recursive = -1;

4.      $page = $this->Page->find('first', array('conditions' => array('id'
         => $data['Page']['id'])));

5.      $revision = array('PagesRevision' => array(

6.            'page_id' => $page['Page']['id'],

7.            'category_id' => $page['Page']['category_id'],

8.            'title' => $page['Page']['title'],
```

```
9.              'body' => $page['Page']['body']

10.          )

11.     );

12.     $this->create();

13.     $this->save($revision);

14. }

15.

16. function deleteRevision($page_id) {

17.     $this->deleteAll(array('page_id' => $page_id), false, false);

18. }

19.

20. function revertPage($id) {

21.     $this->recursive = -1;

22.     $this->id = $id;

23.     $page = $this->read();

24.     // update the page with the current revisions data data

25.     $newData = array('Page' => array(

26.          'id' => $page['PagesRevision']['page_id'],

27.          'category_id' => $page['PagesRevision']['category_id'],

28.          'title' => $page['PagesRevision']['title'],
```

```
29.              'body' => $page['PagesRevision']['body']

30.      )

31.      );

32.  $this->Page->save($newData);

33.  // save the file

34.  App::import('Component', 'File');

35.  $this->File = new FileComponent();

36.  $this->File->saveFile($newData);

37.  }
```

The saveRevision() function retrieves the current page from the database prior to saving it. We proceed to create a new PagesRevision record with this data. This function is performed on every change to our page model data.

The deleteRevision() function performs a deleteAll() on the revision table and removes all revisions for the specified page.

The final function, revertPage(), retrieves the data from the revision. It calls the save function in the page model. After we've saved our page, we import the file component and re-save the file to ensure it is up-to-date.

The next model is the pages comment model. Like the page model above, we updated the belongsTo array for the page relationship. In the pages table, we created a field called pages_comment_count. By adding the counterCache here, CakePHP will automatically maintain the count of comments for us. This change can be seen here:

```
1.   'Page' => array('className' => 'Page',

2.         'foreignKey' => 'page_id',

3.         'conditions' => '',

4.         'fields' => '',

5.         'order' => '',

6.         'counterCache' => true

7.     ),
```

Our final model is the user model. This model is unchanged from "Chapter 5: How to setup Authentication".

If you were to load your web browser and attempt to navigate to any items in the pages controller, you may notice funny things happening. By default, CakePHP has a route in place that maps all links to the pages controller to the display function. Because we have additional functions in our pages controller that we don't want filtered through this function, we need to alter the app\config\routes.php file:

```
1.   <?php

2.   /**

3.   Here, we are connecting '/' (base path) to controller called 'Pages',

4.   its action called 'display', and we pass a param to select the view file

5.   to use (in this case, /app/views/pages/home.ctp)...

6.   */

7.     Router::connect('/', array('controller' => 'pages', 'action' =>
```

```
    'home'));

8.  /**

9.  ...and connect the rest of 'Pages' controller's urls.

10. */

11.     Router::connect('/pages/index', array('controller' => 'pages',
        'action' => 'index'));

12.     Router::connect('/pages/add', array('controller' => 'pages',
        'action' => 'add'));

13.     Router::connect('/pages/edit/*', array('controller' => 'pages',
        'action' => 'edit'));

14.     Router::connect('/pages/delete/*', array('controller' => 'pages',
        'action' => 'delete'));

15.     Router::connect('/pages/home/*', array('controller' => 'pages',
        'action' => 'home'));

16.     Router::connect('/pages/*', array('controller' => 'pages', 'action'
        => 'display'));

17. ?>
```

In the above code, we've told CakePHP to connect "/" to our home() function of the pages controller.

The last line is the same line that CakePHP uses to connect our pages to the display function. Above this line, we've created one route per function in our pages controller.

Our core code is now completed. The next part is to create our various views to provide a visual of the content. This next portion, we will skim over quickly because the focus of this book is not on HTML. We'll touch upon the important parts of the views and I will allow you to make it look pretty! If I haven't said before, I may be a good developer and I do not delude myself into thinking that I'm a good designer, so I'll just leave that part to the experts.

We are going to need a few Javascript libraries, let's take care of those now. To accomplish the drag and drop category management, we'll need those same Jquery libraries we used back in chapter 8. Visit http://jquery.com and download and save both the Jquery and Jquery-UI libraries. These files should be saved to app/webroot/js.

By default, the AJAX helper with CakePHP uses the Prototype library. I'm not a fan of having multiple Javascript libraries in my project; however, as long as we are careful and don't cross them over, we'll be ok. Visit http://www.prototypejs.org/ and download the prototype library. This file should also be saved in the app/webroot/js folder.

Finally, we need to download the FckEditor library. FckEditor is a "What You See Is What You Get" (WYSIWYG) editor that allows users to create HTML content pages without HTML knowledge. Visit http://www.fckeditor.net/ and download the library. These files should be saved in the app/webroot/js folder.

Now that we have our third party downloads taken care of, let's proceed to the views now.

To allow us to navigate through our site, let's create a default layout. Copy the file: cake\libs\view\layouts\default.ctp to app\views\layouts. Once copied, open it up and we will add an extremely basic menu:

```
1.   <ul>

2.      <li><?php echo $html->link('Home', '/');?></li>

3.      <?php if (empty($user_id)):?><li><?php echo $html-
        >link('Register', '/users/add');?></li>

4.      <li><?php echo $html->link('Login', '/users/login');?></li><?php
        else:?><?php if ($is_admin):?><li><?php echo $html->link('Admin',
        '/pages/index');?></li><?php endif;?>

5.      <li><?php echo $html->link('Logout', '/users/logout');?></li>

6.      <?php endif;?>

7.   </ul>
```

The following code should be placed in the "header" <div> under the <h1> tag. As I discussed in the app controller section, we've passed in some user information. We now use that to determine how the menu should be drawn.

We first check if the user id is empty. If it is empty, the user is not logged in. Let's display the register and login links.

If the user is logged in, we proceed to check if they are an admin user. If they are, we display an admin menu item to them. This will take them to the management of pages. Finally we include a logout link to all logged in users.

Our next view is the view that is loaded by default, app/views/pages/home.ctp:

```
1.   <div style="float: left; width: 35%">

2.     <?php echo $this->requestAction('/categories/public_list');?>

3.   </div>

4.   <div style="float: left; width: 65%">

5.     <h1>Pages</h1>

6.     <?php if (!empty($pages)):?><?php foreach ($pages as
       $page):?><div>

7.       <h2><?php echo $html->link($page['Page']['title'], '/pages/' .
         $file->buildPath($page, false));?></h2>

8.       <p><?php echo substr($page['Page']['body'], 0, 150);?></p>

9.       <hr>

10.      <?php

11.        $comments = $page['Page']['pages_comment_count'] . '
           Comment';

12.        if ($page['Page']['pages_comment_count'] <> 1)

13.          $comments .= 's';

14.        echo $html->link($comments, '/pages/' . $file-
           >buildPath($page, false) . '#comments');?>

15.    </div>

16.    <?php endforeach;?><?php else:?><p><em>No pages have been
       added yet.</em></p><?php endif;?>

17.  </div>
```

The following view creates two floating divs. In the first one, we use a requestAction() call to retrieve the list of categories. The second div displays a list of the pages. The title is a link to the full page. We also create a link to the comments pages. This is actually the same page, we just add an anchor link so if there is a lot of content before the comments; it will jump directly to the comment section.

When a page is clicked on, CakePHP will load our statically generated view that is created in our pages controller. It includes the request action call that will display our comments for that page.

Let's review that file now, app\views\pages_comments\index.ctp:

1. `<?php`

2. `echo $javascript->link('prototype');`

3. `echo $javascript->codeBlock('function updateCommentList(page_id) {`

4. `new Ajax.Updater("comments","/HelloWorld_Final/pages_comments/index/" + page_id, {asynchronous:true, evalScripts:true, requestHeaders:["X-Update", "content"]});`

5. `}');`

6. `?>`

7. `<div id="comments">`

8. `<h2><a name="comments"></a><?php __('PagesComments');?></h2>`

9. `<p>`

10. `<?php`

11. $paginator->options(array('update' => 'content', 'indicator' => 'spinner'));

12.   echo $paginator->counter(array(

13.   'format' => __('Page %page% of %pages%, showing %current% records out of %count% total, starting on record %start%, ending on %end%', true)

14.   ));

15.   ?></p>

16.   <?php foreach ($pagesComments as $pagesComment):?>

17.   <?php echo $pagesComment['User']['last_name'] . ', ' . $pagesComment['User']['first_name']; ?>

18.   <?php echo $pagesComment['PagesComment']['comment']; ?>

19.   <?php echo $pagesComment['PagesComment']['created']; ?>

20.   <?php if (!empty($user_id) && $user_id == $pagesComment['PagesComment']['user_id']):?><?php echo $ajax->link(__('Delete', true), array('action'=>'delete', $pagesComment['PagesComment']['id'], $pagesComment['PagesComment']['page_id']), array('complete' => 'updateCommentList(' . $page_id . ')'), sprintf(__('Are you sure you want to delete # %s?', true), $pagesComment['PagesComment']['id'])); ?><?php endif;?>

21.   <?php endforeach; ?>

22.   <div id="newcomment"></div>

23.   <div class="paging">

24.   <?php echo $paginator->prev('<< '.__('previous', true), array(),

null, array('class'=>'disabled'));?>

25. | <?php echo $paginator->numbers();?>

26.   <?php echo $paginator->next(__('next', true).' >>', array(),
null, array('class'=>'disabled'));?>

27.   </div>

28.   <div class="actions">

29.   <ul>

30.   <?php if (!empty($user_id)):?><li><?php echo $ajax-
>link(__('New PagesComment', true), 'add/' . $page_id,
array('update' => 'newcomment')); ?></li><?php else:?>

31.   <li>To add a comment, <?php echo $html->link('sign up',
'/users/add');?> or <?php echo $html->link('login',
'/users/login');?></li><?php endif;?>

32.   </ul>

33.   </div>

34. </div>

This file was originally created from the bakery. We've altered it slightly. The first thing we do is include the prototype library. The next portion of Javascript code performs an AJAX request that reloads the comment list. This function is called after deleting and adding a comment.

The original baked file included an $html->link() to add a new comment. We've altered this to use the AJAX helper. When this link is clicked, it will load the contents of app\views\pages_comments\add.ctp through AJAX and insert the HTML into the div called "newcomment".

If the user is not logged in, we display the register and sign up links instead of the add link.

Next is our aforementioned add.ctp file:

```
1.   <div class="pagesComments form">

2.   <?php echo $form->create('PagesComment');?>

3.   <fieldset>

4.      <legend><?php __('Add PagesComment');?></legend>

5.      <?php

6.         echo $form->input('page_id', array('type' => 'hidden'));

7.         echo $form->input('comment');

8.      ?>

9.   </fieldset>

10.  <?php

11.  echo $ajax->submit('Add', array('url' => 'add', 'complete' =>
     'updateCommentList(' . $this->data['PagesComment']['page_id'] .
     ')'));

12.  echo $form->end();

13.  ?>

14.  </div>
```

We've made one major change from the bakery. Prior to the $form->end() call, we've created an AJAX submit button. Clicking this button will call the add() function in the pages controller through AJAX. When it is done, it will call our updateCommentList() function that will reload the list of comments.

The next two files are our user's views: add.ctp and login.ctp. These files are unchanged from Chapter 5, so we won't include them here.

Our last public file is a category listing, app\views\categories\public_listing.ctp:

```
1.  <?php echo $this->element('draw_category_link', array('data' =>
    $categories)); ?>
```

Did I overwhelm you with all of that code? As you may notice, we simply include our draw category element that we created in chapter 8. The only difference is we actually made a new element called draw_category_link. This file functions the exact same way as the original draw_category file, except that we've linked our categories to filter the list of pages.

Therefore, our app\views\elements\draw_category_link.ctp does the following:

```
1.  <?php if ($data): ?><ul>

2.  <?php foreach ($data as $category): ?><li id="category_<?php echo
    $category['Category']['id']; ?>"><span><?php echo $html-
    >link($category['Category']['name'], '/pages/home/' .
    $category['Category']['name']); ?> (<?php echo
    $category['Category']['page_count'];?> page<?php if
    ($category['Category']['page_count'] <> 1):?>s<?php
    endif;?>)</span>

3.  <?php echo $this->element('draw_category_link', array('data' =>
    $category['children'])); ?>
```

4.   </li><?php endforeach; ?>

5.   </ul><?php endif; ?>

As you can see, we've created a link to /pages/home/<category name>. We've also included in brackets the count of pages for this category.

This now concludes the public portion of our views.

The admin side is very basic. Most of our code was created by the bakery and will remain untouched.   The admin area consists of the following views:

- app\views\categories\index.ctp – unchanged from chapter 8

- app\views\categories\add.ctp – unchanged from chapter 8

- app\views\pages\index.ctp – one small change discussed below

- app\views\pages\add.ctp – inclusion of FckEditor for HTML style

- app\views\pages\edit.ctp – inclusion of FckEditor for HTML style

- app\views\pages_revisions\index.ctp – removed unneeded links and added a link to revert to this revision

- app\views\pages_revisions\view.ctp – added new link to revert to this revision

Below is the small change to the app\views\pages\index.ctp:

Inside of the <td class="actions"> we've replaced the view link with the following:

1. <?php echo $html->link(__('View Revisions', true), array('controller' => 'pages_revisions', 'action'=>'index', $page['Page']['id'])); ?>

This link will take the user to listing of revisions for that particular page. From there the user may view or revert their changes.

Our pages add and edit files are very similar and contain the same code at the top of each to initialize the FckEditor:

1. <?php echo $javascript->link('fckeditor/fckeditor', false); ?>

2. <?php echo $javascript->codeBlock('

3. window.onload = function() {

4.   var oFCKeditor = new FCKeditor("PageBody") ;

5.   oFCKeditor.BasePath = "/HelloWorld_Final/js/fckeditor/" ;

6.   oFCKeditor.ReplaceTextarea() ;

7. }

8. ', array('safe' => false, 'inline' => false)); ?>

The first line of code includes our Javascript library. The second portion creates a window onload function that instantiates our fck editor.

The final two pages in the revisions view include the following link to call the revert process:

1. ```php
   <?php echo $html->link(__('Revert', true), array('action'=>'revert',
   $pagesRevision['PagesRevision']['id'])); ?>
   ```

SUMMARY

That completes our CMS. I'll leave the styling and finishing touches up to you. At this point we should have a decent functioning CMS created in CakePHP.

Note: To maintain our focus on certain areas of CakePHP our CMS is not 100% ready for commercialization. More error handling and duplicate checking of categories and pages would be required to make it more versatile.

This concludes our CakePHP learning in this book. I hope you've enjoyed it and have fallen in love with CakePHP as I have! Now, get out there are start creating all of your great website ideas rapidly.

If you are looking for new articles and tutorials, don't forget to visit my blog at: http://www.endyourif.com
   ```

CHAPTER 13

UPGRADING CAKEPHP

As I discussed during the preface of this book, all of the code above was originally written with version 1.2 of CakePHP. In this chapter we are going to demonstrate a basic process to upgrading your version of CakePHP.

OBJECTIVES

- Define why we should upgrade

- Upgrade CakePHP

- Ensure we remove deprecated functions

The upgrade process usually should be pretty straight forward. Sometimes, depending on the size of the project, it might be time consuming, but it should still be straight forward. Don't let the size of your project discourage you from upgrading as there are many valuable reasons to upgrade.

WHEN TO UPGRADE

If your project is a "living" project, e.g. keeps changing and growing in functionality on a regular basis, it's best to perform frequent upgrades. I would go as far as upgrading with every new stable release. E.g. if you are using 1.3.7 stable and 1.3.8 stable comes out I would work into your development schedule the time to upgrade. A minor upgrade like this should be minimal.

MAKING THE UPGRADE EASIER

To ensure a smooth upgrade, there are several things you can do that will make the process simpler.

The first is the simplest. Upgrade frequently; don't wait for a major change, e.g. version 1.2 to 1.3. Historically, and for good reason, when CakePHP does a major upgrade like this, they add and remove functionality; often times deprecating existing functionality. Typically as versions evolve, they will start to work towards these major changes. Staying alert and on top of the changes will make things easier.

The second is a little bit harder, but not much. Be sure to always follow CakePHP's standards while developing. If you follow their guidelines and principals, upgrading should take no effort at all.

The third is the most difficult, but probably the best. Write automated tests, whether they are web tests or unit tests, having these tests will make upgrading the easiest process of all. Automated testing will tell you exactly which page, controller, or function is no longer working properly. Without automated testing, each time you upgrade you will need to perform manual testing on your entire site to ensure no issues arose during the upgrade process. It might not sound difficult, but this is the first place mistakes will start to happen.

WHY SHOULD YOU UPGRADE

Stability, reliability, security, and enhancements. With each release, CakePHP becomes a stronger and better framework.

In a recent blog post, I put this too the test comparing versions 1.2 to 1.3 to 2.0 and the results were astonishing. From 1.2 to version 1.3 there was an impressive 300 millisecond improvement per request. In today's society, every millisecond counts. This benchmark test is only referring to the weight of the framework itself; it doesn't take into consideration the improvements with models, helpers, etc...which would probably make the times even more significant.

HOW TO UPGRADE

Finally, the good stuff, let's upgrade our CakePHP. Way back in Chapter 2, you may recall the screenshot shows version 1.3.7. Originally that would show a version 1.2.x version. Since it was originally created, the version of CakePHP has been upgraded without changing any significant code!

To begin, visit www.cakephp.org and download the latest stable release of the version you would like to upgrade too.

Once downloaded, unzip this code into your "htdocs" or "webroot" folder (like we did in chapter 2).

Load this in your web browser and ensure everything is working correctly.

Next, we need to bring our code into the new version of CakePHP. We are going to copy the entire "app" folder from our existing project, to our new project.

Wait! There are a few exceptions. The following files are actually CakePHP core files and they should remain the same for the version we downloaded:

- app\index.php

- app\webroot\css.php

- app\webroot\test.php

- app\webroot\index.php

So copy your entire "app" folder with the exclusion of the above four files.

The next thing we need to do is review the migration guide. Visit http://book.cakephp.org and under the Appendices there should be a migration guide to follow. Read through this document to ensure anything that you were previously doing isn't deprecated or changed in this version.

For example, I was using the Session Component without including it in my project because in version 1.2 it was automatically included; however, in version 1.3 it wasn't. This was a simple fix, I just add to update my components array in my app_controller and everything started working!

Depending on the details of your project, you may or may not have more work to do. Don't worry, the improvements far outweigh the time spent!

SUMMARY

I hope this special bonus chapter involving upgrading your CakePHP website has been useful and eased the pain in the decision making progress to upgrade or not.

Keep on building websites fast!

www.ingramcontent.com/pod-product-compliance
Lightning Source LLC
LaVergne TN
LVHW022319060326
832902LV00020B/3550